Praise for *Collabo*

"I am so grateful to Heather for sharing her insights, expertise, and wisdom through the pages of *Collaborative Confidence*. I have been hungry for a concise, easy and entertaining book with practical advice and examples of ways to support, develop and advance women at our company. Thank you, Heather!"

Lynne Whiteford, Vice President Talent Management
GoodRX

"In today's ever-changing business environment, women are held to a much higher standard. Dr. Backstrom's book *Collaborative Confidence* gives women a clear path forward. The concepts in the book are elegant in their simplicity and gives the reader a practical approach to being introspective, using their voice, and making an impact. Activate, Amplify, and Accelerate are critical steps for women leaders and the book beautifully lays them out with clarity and effectiveness."

Dr. Gabriella Miramontes, Assistant Clinical Professor, Doctoral
Programs, Special Projects, and Belonging Initiatives
Pepperdine University

"Every situation is a learning experience. *Collaborative Confidence* is a reminder that what you take from every experience helps you grow and helps other women do the same."

Michelle Vielma, Vice President of Advertising
Advertising industry

"*Collaborative Confidence* offers a refreshing perspective that every woman leader should read."

Sonya Makunga, Head of Real Estate Legal
Major entertainment studio

Collaborative CONFIDENCE

How women leaders can activate
self-awareness, amplify their authentic
talents, and accelerate workplace change

DR. HEATHER BACKSTROM

ISBN: 978-1-647046-51-4 (paperback)
ISBN: 978-1-647046-50-7 (ebook)

Unless otherwise indicated, all names, characters, businesses, places, events, and incidents
in this book are a product of the author's experience, research, or imagination. Any
resemblance to actual persons, living or dead, or actual events is purely coincidental.

Although every effort has been made to ensure the information was correct at time of press,
and while this publication is designed to provide accurate information, the author assumes
no responsibility for errors, inaccuracies, omissions, or other inconsistencies herein and
hereby disclaims any liability to any party for any loss, damage, or disruption caused by
errors or omissions, whether the result of negligence, accident, or any other cause.

The information is for educational purposes and not intended as a substitute for professional
services including, but not limited to, legal, financial, or psychotherapy. The author
makes no guarantees, representations or warranties of any kind, express or implied,
concerning the level of success you may experience by following the ideas, advice, or
strategies contained in this book. Results differ for each individual. The illustrations, ideas,
strategies, and examples are not intended to represent or guarantee similar results. Any
use of this information is at your own risk. The author shall not be held liable for any loss
or damage allegedly arising from any suggestion or information contained in this book.

To my Grandma Backstrom and Grandma Frost.
Two incredibly strong women in their own distinctive ways.

Table of Contents

Acknowledgements

While writing in and of itself may be a solo act, writing a book certainly is not. I'm grateful to the countless people who supported and encouraged me, and provided their time, advice and expertise. They have been instrumental in bringing this book to life. My editor, Kathy Meis, and her entire team at Bublish have been extraordinary to work with. Kathy's professional expertise, steadfast dedication and supportive spirit guided me throughout the entire process from beginning to end. The remarkable team at Bublish, too, have ensured a smooth, enjoyable, and professional experience.

Along the way my mom, Mary K., encouraged me and read several chapters of the book, giving her feedback and thoughts. My niece, Spencer Gonzales, with her artistic talent was instrumental in creating the cover design with me. Several people read early versions of the book and offered invaluable feedback including Annissa Deshpande, Dr. Michele Nealon, Johanna Torres, Allison Leung, and Karen Palmersheim. I interviewed a number of people whose perspectives were woven into the book's content: Sarah Leung, Dena Rothmann, Lindsay Francis, Elsa Sham, Donina Ifurung, Ismenia Monchez Moreno, Cedar Carter, Skyler Mattson, Jane Finette, Lidia Soto-Harmon, and Teresa Shafer. For their generous support and help, I also want to thank Mark Welches, Janis Clementz, Natalie Barron, Mary Ellen Derro, Dr. Gabriella Miramontes, Dr. Aasiyah

Ghazi, Vanessa Jahn, Dr. Sonya Sharififard, Dr. Renee Dorn, Dr. Larry Keene, and the Pepperdine University community.

I also want to thank everyone I've worked with across the years including clients, workshop participants, colleagues, and bosses. I'm also grateful for the students I've had in the classes I've taught at the University of Redlands. All of these individuals have contributed to my professional and personal development.

It's with a grateful heart that I extend my sincere thanks to everyone who helped and supported me. Thank for you for bringing *Collaborative Confidence* to life.

Foreword

We have been deeply entrenched in the topic of leadership for decades; informally as we gather in our workplace hallways to reflect on a colleague's or executive's style of engagement and formally through organizationally focused research. These conversations and formal studies have produced much about what we have come to accept as optimal leadership. We intuitively are aware of when we are in the presence of great leadership. There is an aura we notice, a sense of contagion we can quite easily reflect upon, and a feeling of being motivated and inspired that energizes us. Yet, it is only recently that true progress has been made in understanding what is unique and valuable about women's leadership. Thankfully, we are moving past the elementary comparisons of gender specific leadership, and there is a growing acceptance that women leaders are, in fact, effective and powerful.

Thankfully also, we are maturing in our willingness to embrace what it means to be a woman leader and not negating a woman in a leadership position simply because of any negative biases about the female gender. In addition, we are moving past the pressure for women to lead in alignment with the male norm and starting to celebrate what are uniquely women's strengths in leadership.

Collaborative Confidence is a heartening testament to this current state. Heather eloquently discusses women's leadership from a personal advancement and wellness perspective that I find refreshing. The pages within celebrate what is unique about women, not in a manner that seeks to justify women's leadership, nor compare it to that of male leadership. Rather, Heather speaks directly to women who are leaders and who are comfortable owning their strength and power. Through stories, research, and her experience as an executive coach, she invites women to reflect on how they can magnify what is already natural for them and challenges them to step toward areas in which they can improve. In a refreshing manner, she also invites women to learn from each other and never forget to extend a hand backward to the women leaders coming behind them.

Heather coined the term Collaborative Confidence and describes it as "I'm responsible for my own confidence, and I'm responsible for helping other women with theirs". When fully understood and enacted, it provides an opportunity for reciprocal engagement among women and can be leveraged with a group, one-on-one, or both. Collaborative Confidence elevates a woman leader's level of self-awareness, provides opportunities for leadership action in alignment with a woman's personal values, fosters executive presence, encourages individual and group advocacy, champions other women, and even provides a platform upon which organizations can better adapt to the needs of women in the workplace.

Collaborative Confidence is built upon three essential pillars: Activate, Amplify, and Accelerate. As with all personal growth processes, the Activate pillar is about a woman doing her inner work: becoming self-aware, taming her inner critics, finding and empowering her inner champion, owning her strengths, and living true to her core values. The Amplify pillar is a logical extension of Activate in that a woman learns how to become more visible at a personal and public level and reach out to help other women do the same. She elevates her leadership impact because she is not only more self-aware but also crisper in her leadership through executive presence, more adept at seizing the opportunities that come her way, and is proud to own her accomplishments. She is also deeply invested in amplifying other women too. The power of the mutual reciprocity of women amplifying each other is center stage. The Accelerate pillar acknowledges that women cannot succeed alone, that their organizations also have a crucial role in elevating women's leadership. Organizations must evolve to create human-centric cultures through sponsorship, flexible work environments, equal pay, and addressing burnout.

Women leaders instinctively understand the importance of the Activate, Amplify, and Accelerate pillars. *Collaborative Confidence* brings that understanding to life and encourages women to always extend self-awareness into self-action, elevating the power of leadership confidence and impact in the process.

Michele Nealon, PsyD
President
The Chicago School of Professional Psychology

Introduction

Have you ever felt stuck in your job? I know the feeling, and it's not a good one. Maybe you like the company you work for but want a different role. Maybe you long for a lateral move or an upward promotion. Or maybe you yearn for a job at a different company. Regardless, you crave work that feeds your soul, honors your core values, and leverages your strengths. You want to be authentic and make a genuine impact. Yet, despite this gnawing desire, you're stuck.

Maybe you're at the same point I found myself at many years ago, basically sleepwalking through work. Sure, you get the work done and you do it well, but inside, you feel empty. You've achieved great success, are well respected, and are highly valued. The organization you work for does not want to lose you. You're appreciated and get praise from your team, colleagues, and boss. On the outside, things look rosy, but on the inside, you're wilting. Maybe you want to lead bigger and bolder projects, lead larger teams, or manage a more substantial portfolio. Maybe you want to shift into a different role that aligns more closely with your unique talents—like a move from marketing to government relations, or from finance to cybersecurity. Or maybe you want to do completely different work, as I did at the time. I was stuck in human resources and wanted to be an executive coach.

If this sounds familiar, you're not alone. I lived my version of this painful struggle for years. It was hard to get up and go to work when I knew deep down I wanted to do something else. I felt stuck. Then, an unforeseen and painful event propelled me into action.

I began my professional career working in corporate human resources as a recruiter. At first, I enjoyed it and felt fulfilled, especially when it resulted in finding just the right person for just the right job. It seemed almost magical when the hiring manager and the job candidate matched up perfectly. Of course, it wasn't magic; it came from working closely with the hiring manager to learn about the skills and qualifications they were looking for. It also came from getting to know the qualifications of the job candidates and establishing a friendly rapport with them. As my time in human resources progressed, my experience increased. Eventually, I spent time in employee relations work, which included managing employee performance issues, writing written warnings, devising company reorganizations, conducting internal investigations, and terminating people's employment. For quite a while, the work was interesting. Over time, though, its appeal faded. I suppose it's not unusual to enjoy a particular profession for a period of time, only to find its appeal wane as the years go by. As I began to gradually realize human resources work was no longer for me, I set my sights on becoming an executive coach.

I enrolled in a professional coaching school called the Co-Active Training Institute (CTI). I'll never forget my first CTI class; the whole experience hit me with such force. I finally felt at home. I still remember how energized and enthusiastic I felt. I could hardly wait to start coaching! In 2006, I finished the program and became a full-fledged coach—at least on paper. I didn't have a job in the field and was still working in human resources. Luckily, I was able to incorporate a little coaching into my day-to-day human resources job. Most of the time, though, I was still dealing with people's performance problems, writing formal warnings, conducting workplace investigations, firing people, and navigating company reorganization plans. I was depleted and couldn't find a way out. Then, the universe intervened with a swift kick. I made a mistake at work. While I owned up to it, I found myself on the receiving end of one of those warnings I had written to other people so many times. Ouch! It was that experience, fueled by my love of coaching, that finally propelled me to quit. Without a single coaching client lined up, I walked out of my human resources job and never looked back.

Today, I'm happy to say I'm a full-time executive coach. The intelligent, capable, experienced women leaders I am honored to coach represent a wide range of industries, including financial services, biotech, retail, healthcare, aerospace, municipalities, entertainment, media, higher education, legal services, commercial real estate, and nonprofit. They mainly work as vice presidents and C-suite executives, overseeing substantial portfolios of people and assets. They have a lot of work on their plates and juggle a heavy load of expectations. These are the women for whom I wrote *Collaborative Confidence*, which is based on my unique approach to coaching.

The term "Collaborative Confidence" emerged from my coaching experiences with women leaders and my intuition. Both showed me that women are relational creatures who need confidence to succeed and crave connection and collaboration. As I explored these ideas further, the concept of Collaborative Confidence dropped right into my consciousness. It was a lightbulb moment. I knew I was onto something when I shared it with other women. They were instantly drawn in, having a visceral reaction to the mere words "Collaborative Confidence." This happened without them even knowing what the words meant. With their interest piqued, the women literally leaned forward, their eyes bright, saying, "Oh, I love the sound of that. Tell me more." When I shared the term's meaning, they immediately related.

Collaborative Confidence means "I'm responsible for my own confidence, and I'm responsible for helping other women with theirs." They loved it! Collaborative Confidence is reciprocal, relational, inclusive, and connective.

I can think of no better example to illustrate Collaborative Confidence than the women cabinet leaders during former president Obama's first administration. To get their ideas and voices heard, these women banded together to create a strategy they called "amplification." In meetings, whenever a woman made a statement, gave an opinion, or offered an idea, the other women in the room made sure it was heard loud and clear. They'd repeat it and redirect the conversation back to the woman who'd made the statement. They were committed to amplifying her and giving her full credit. These behaviors epitomize the spirit of Collaborative Confidence.

The beauty of Collaborative Confidence is that it's pliable. While the women of the Obama administration amplified each other's voices in meetings, Collaborative Confidence also applies anytime you are uncertain, have a tough decision to make, need to take a stand, or are faced with risk or adversity. In such times, you can rely on other women to help you think through the issues at hand and support you as you move forward. You can engage in Collaborative Confidence with a group, one-on-one, or both. It's really up to you and the situation. I'm fortunate to have several trusted women friends and colleagues with whom I regularly engage in Collaborative Confidence.

I recall a recent time when I needed to have a tough, unpleasant conversation with a client. My nerves buzzed, even though I knew it was the right thing to do. In making the decision to talk with the client, I relied on a close female colleague. She helped me clarify my thoughts, sort through my feelings, make sense of my fears, and plan my message. Before talking with her, I was a jumbled mess inside.

She helped me regain my footing and have the confidence to speak effectively with the client. Afterward, she was there to support and commend me for not shying away from a difficult situation. She also helped me learn from the experience. Throughout our relationship, I've done the same for her when she faced uncertainty or held herself back from pursuing opportunities. This is just one of many examples from my own life that demonstrate Collaborative Confidence.

The distinctive talents of women leaders I've experienced is also backed by research. According to a study conducted by Caliper (a Princeton-based management consulting firm) and Aurora (a London-based organization that advances women's leadership), "Women leaders . . . were found to be more empathic and flexible, as well as stronger in interpersonal skills than their male counterparts." Herb Greenberg, president and chief executive officer of Caliper, adds, "These qualities combine to create a leadership style that is inclusive, open, consensus building, collaborative and collegial." These characteristics tie right into what it means to engage in Collaborative Confidence. The story of the women from Obama's administration and my own example demonstrate empathy, inclusivity, consensus, collegiality, confidence, and courage. Building your confidence by trying new behaviors and adjusting your mindset takes courage. There is no guarantee how things will turn out. You may feel unsure along the way. That's okay. Lean on other women for support on the journey. That's the beauty of Collaborative Confidence, which can guide you to:

- become more self-aware,
- work and live in alignment with your values,
- showcase your unique skills and talents and those of other women,
- foster your executive presence,

- demonstrate your impact,
- enhance your influence,
- embrace the best opportunities,
- encourage and advocate for other women,
- call attention to the talents and skills of other women,
- be a champion for other women,
- and bring about meaningful and substantive change for women in the workplace.

When women engage in Collaborative Confidence, they are naturally truer to themselves and help other women to be the same. Through the stories and research presented in this book, we'll unpack the three pillars of Collaborative Confidence: Activate, Amplify, and Accelerate.

> **ACTIVATE.** With this pillar, the focus is on you— your self-awareness, inner champion, core values, and strengths. Think of engaging with these chapters as doing your inner work. With this pillar, you'll learn to activate various qualities that make you the unique, capable leader you are.

> **AMPLIFY.** This pillar is about making your impact more visible, while doing the same for other women. The Amplify pillar gets to the heart of the reciprocal nature of Collaborative Confidence. You'll learn to enhance your executive presence, seize more opportunities, spotlight your accomplishments, and elevate your leadership—all while doing the same for other women by highlighting their impact and

advancing their accomplishments. The Amplify pillar brings greater prominence to you and other women.

ACCELERATE. This pillar looks outward to the bigger topic of women's leadership today and how organizations play a vital role. It examines the responsibility organizations have to create more human-centric corporate cultures and ultimately transform the world, one company at a time.

This book is for brilliant, talented, successful women leaders, just like you. I wrote it because I no longer want women to doubt themselves or hold themselves back. I also don't want women to endure the kind of struggle I did when they know they want something different from their current career. I want women to stand strong in their self-belief and feel confident about how they can move forward together. With that sense of steady confidence, women can feel comfortable expanding their horizons, taking risks, and making an impact in their own unique, authentic way.

I also wrote this book because I have witnessed and experienced the powerful, undeniable force of women supporting women. When women unite and amplify each other, the effect is nothing short of remarkable. On the individual level, women benefit because they know, with complete assuredness, that other women are in their corner—and not just in their corner, but actively looking for ways to amplify them. On a collective level, amplification changes and benefits the whole. When groups of women amplify each other, the effect acts as a multiplier that positively changes the workplace. This was so beautifully evidenced by the women cabinet leaders during former president Obama's first administration.

My hope is that this book will inspire you to weave together a happy and fulfilling life and career. As we explore self-awareness, inner champions and critics, values, strengths, executive presence, corporate cultures, and more, I hope you'll discover and create your own gorgeous life tapestry—one that is a true reflection of your passions and goals. And, as you strengthen your confidence, I hope it becomes natural for you to amplify other talented women and live a life of Collaborative Confidence.

SECTION I

Activate

BECOME MORE SELF-AWARE

Self-aware women are more assured and intentional about their emotions, behaviors, actions, and choices. They are also more willing to share and defend their ideas and principles. Even when things get tough, self-aware women have the fortitude to stay true to themselves and their values. These are all strong leadership qualities.

Chapter 1

Enhance Self-Awareness as a Competitive Advantage

Sophia, a successful, highly regarded senior vice president of finance, loves her work. But lately, she has been feeling out of sorts. Something is off, causing a knot in her stomach. First, she noticed she was not included in the cross-organizational project team charged with selecting the company's new digital-strategy vendor. Normally, she'd be highly involved with such a significant project. The knot in her stomach tightened more when she wasn't asked to attend the entire board of directors and executive officers' annual retreat. She was only asked to attend a portion to present the company's financials. In her five years with the organization, she had always attended the entire retreat. After all, she's only one rung below the executive level. She's worried, uncertain, and having trouble sleeping. She wants to shake it off, but none of it makes sense.

Sophia is a whiz with numbers and excels at financial analysis. She gets complimented for her ability to take complex numbers and turn them into meaningful information. She prides herself on this. She also enjoys collaborating with others to reach common goals.

She likes being part of a team, especially those that require analytical thinking. Given all this, she wonders, *Why the change?*

Perhaps you can relate to Sophia's story. I know I can. Something feels off, and your mind starts chattering. *Charlotte decided to leave me out without a good reason. Nathan doesn't respect my opinions and expertise.* Maybe you're like me and blame yourself. *Clearly, I'm not good enough. I'm in over my head.* Even though we all know knee-jerk responses like these aren't helpful, it's hard not to go down the rabbit hole of self-doubt and criticism. This kind of internal dialogue almost always leads to a downward spiral of negativity and blame that's hard to escape. That is, unless you put concentrated effort into shifting your mindset.

When my clients are in a negativity spiral, I've found two coaching skills to be most effective: listening and being present. Simply being there for a client, listening to them and being present for them, can help relax them and reverse the downward spiral. I encourage them to tune out the noise and look inward. I show them how to use self-awareness to regain their footing. The good news is self-awareness is always accessible. You don't have to pull a book off your shelf, look something up on the internet, or buy a course. It's always at your disposal. But becoming self-aware takes time, discipline, and attention. And believe me, sometimes the process can be painful, full of tears and courageous self-confession. But the payoff is tremendous and definitely worth the work.

People generally believe they are more self-aware than they are. In a fascinating study published in 2018 by the *Harvard Business Review*, researcher Tasha Eurich looked at nearly five thousand participants and found that while most people believe they are self-aware, many are not. In truth, self-awareness is rather uncommon. According to Eurich's findings, only 10 to 15 percent of the study's participants fit

COLLABORATIVE CONFIDENCE | 5

the criteria for self-awareness. Not good, right? But there's an opportunity in that dismal statistic: you can stand out from the crowd by boosting your self-awareness. Think of it as a competitive advantage in today's whirling job market. I often talk with clients about self-awareness as having two sides. On one side is what you perceive about yourself (internal self-awareness), and on the other is what others perceive about you (external self-awareness). Eurich's research explains that internal self-awareness includes how clearly you see your strengths, values, and reactions and is associated with enhanced job satisfaction and overall happiness. External self-awareness, on the other hand, reveals that people who understand how they are perceived by others are more skilled at showing empathy and considering others' perspectives. Her research also shows that when leaders see themselves in the same way as their employees, their employees "tend to have a better relationship with them, feel more satisfied with them, and see them as more effective in general."

You might be surprised to learn that self-awareness is also tied to a healthy bottom line. Korn Ferry looked at 486 publicly traded companies and found that companies with a greater percentage of self-aware employees consistently outperformed those with a lower percentage. A study by Green Peak Partners in collaboration with Cornell University found "that 'results-at-all-costs' executives actually diminish the bottom line, especially over time, while self-aware leaders with strong interpersonal skills deliver better financial results."

The level of self-awareness also impacts team performance. A study by researchers Erich C. Dierdorff and Robert S. Rubin shows that high self-awareness among members means a team is more likely to function effectively, perform well, and be more effective at decision-making, coordination, and conflict management. All this research reinforces that self-awareness is key to differentiating yourself as a leader.

Now, let's go back to Sophia, the senior vice president we met at the beginning of the chapter. No wilting flower, she was not about to lose any more sleep over these mysterious events. *What's going on below the surface?* she wondered. Determined to get answers, she took matters into her own hands. She was familiar with the power of self-awareness because she had read Eurich's *Harvard Business Review* article, so she started there. With courage and resolve, she took steps to become more self-aware—both internally and externally. Sitting at her dining-room table one evening with a cup of hot tea, she took out a piece of paper and her favorite pen and wrote down her thoughts, allowing them to flow organically. *Maybe they want to get rid of me and this is the first step. Maybe I'm not good enough. What's wrong with them—don't they see my value? I've worked so hard for so long and they're sidelining me for no reason. They don't want me at the retreat so they can be in the limelight in front of the board.* With every stroke of her pen, her frustration intensified. She could feel the knot in her stomach tighten. She became teary-eyed while documenting her flood of emotions—sadness, loneliness, discouragement, dejection, frustration, and doubt.

She took a sip of tea and several long, deep breaths to center herself. Then, she read all her thoughts out loud. For the first time, she realized they were almost all negative. *No wonder I'm so anxious and can't sleep,* she thought. She read through the list again and realized the weight of her thoughts and feelings. They were suffocating her. She wanted to get out of her negativity spiral, which meant she had to take action. From that moment on, she paid more attention to her thoughts. Each time negative chatter started in her head, she changed her thoughts to something more positive or at least neutral. It wasn't easy; it took discipline and focus. Still, she was determined not to let negative thoughts get the best of her.

She soon realized that stopping her negative thoughts also alleviated her feelings of anger, frustration, and sadness. It was refreshing not to carry those troublesome feelings around anymore. Tuning in to her physical sensations, she realized that when she thought negatively about the situation, the knot in her stomach showed up. By engaging in deep breathing, she was able to calm these unpleasant physical sensations. Ultimately, she was able to think more clearly and feel better again. She even slept better.

It was a great start, but Sophia knew she also had to become more externally self-aware. She mustered up the courage to seek out feedback from her boss and several trusted colleagues. From those conversations, she learned that sometimes she can come across as too forthright, leaving people feeling alienated. She also learned that her financial wizardry can sometimes cause her to be overly focused on the numbers, losing sight of the bigger picture. While the feedback stung and took time to digest, it helped her understand herself from other people's perspectives. This new awareness helped her adjust her behaviors.

While Sophia is still forthright, she now leaves plenty of room for dialogue by asking questions, soliciting input, and focusing on points of agreement. Today, her natural frankness is balanced with openness and curiosity. Additionally, to avoid getting lost in the numbers, she steps back to ask herself how they relate to the bigger picture. Now that her sometimes myopic focus on the numbers is out in the open, she and her boss even joke about it.

Because she took her self-awareness quest to heart, disarmed her negative thinking, tended to her feelings, calmed her physical sensations, and made adjustments to her outward behaviors, Sophia became a more valuable leader. Others in the organization noticed her positive behavioral changes and professional growth. She recalls one day in particular when both the CEO and a colleague from another division commented on the positive changes they'd seen in her. That encouragement put wind in her sails. Her hard work was paying off. Today, Sophia leads cross-organizational project teams and is once again included in the board and executive officers' retreat.

Sophia's story, along with a growing body of research, demonstrates that self-awareness is a competitive leadership advantage. However, it's not enough to focus on only internal or only external self-awareness. To be an effective, authentic, and truly self-aware leader, you must boost both. Let's explore them both in further detail.

Internal Self-Awareness

Internal self-awareness is how you perceive yourself, including your strengths and values. When your strengths and values are crystal clear and serve as your daily guideposts, you're truly living a self-aware life. This beautifully woven combination of your unique strengths and values fills you with purpose and fulfillment. Conversely, when you put your strengths and values to the wayside, you feel unhappy and discouraged. That's what I experienced during my last few years working in corporate America. I found it hard to get up every morning to go to a job that felt so polar opposite from my strengths and values. While I did my best to infuse them into my work, it wasn't enough to alleviate my unhappiness. Let's hear from a former client of mine who had a similar experience.

When I met Yolanda, she had successfully risen through the ranks at a national financial institution and made it all the way to vice president. She excelled at her job, was proud of what she had accomplished, and was highly regarded. Despite that, she confided in me, with tears in her eyes, that she was miserable. It was a tough, toxic environment, but for many years, she'd let the size and stability of her paycheck and the company's perks keep her there. With some hesitation and regret, she admitted to me she enjoyed the comfortable lifestyle her paycheck afforded. She had a beautiful home with an amazing view and drove a luxury car. She took vacations to many interesting places and adorned her home with treasured photos and mementos. However, all the while, the work environment continued to take a toll on her values of humility, empathy, and kindness. To make the situation more complicated, Yolanda's job allowed her to use her strengths every day—strategic thinking, driving for results, being an exceptional communicator, navigating change, and influencing others. She beamed as she told me how great it felt to use her strengths. It was what she most enjoyed about her job. She had also built a strong, cohesive team full of people who supported and respected one another and produced high-quality work. Yolanda cared deeply for her team and, to the best of her abilities, protected them from the executive team's toxicity. This only made it more difficult for her to think about leaving.

"I'm so conflicted," she told me anxiously.

As I coached her, she unearthed the many complex layers of this catch-22. She came to realize the generous compensation and perks didn't offset her inner conflicts about the toxicity of her job. Eventually, she left the organization for work that nourishes her soul and honors her values while still playing to her strengths. Her new self-awareness allowed her to see beyond the present, resolve her internal battles, and move toward a more fulfilling and happier life.

Hopefully, it's now clear *why* you should strive to develop internal self-awareness. Now, let's turn our attention to the *how*. I often point the busy leaders I coach toward quick and simple techniques to heighten their self-awareness anytime and anywhere.

MIND YOUR THOUGHTS. At any moment, in any situation, you can tune in to your thoughts. Are they positive or negative? Constructive or destructive? Do they feel energizing or depleting? When you find yourself caught up in a negative thought, stop it in its tracks like Sophia did. Literally think of something else—your favorite song, the book you're reading, the view from your window. On the surface, interrupting your negative thoughts may sound easy, but as Sophia learned, it takes discipline. In fact, research cited in *Psychology Today* indicates that the vast majority of our thoughts are negative. With that kind of volume, it takes focused, steadfast attention to stop your negative thoughts. Rest assured, the act of minding your mind is a solid first step toward self-awareness.

ASSESS YOUR FEELINGS. Your feelings and thoughts are connected. Tune in to how your thoughts shape your feelings. Notice how negative thoughts make you feel emotions such as agitation, discouragement, and worry. Conversely, notice the effect of positive thoughts. They can make you feel enthusiastic, passionate, and curious, for example. Recall how Sophia realized the dynamic between her thoughts and feelings. During your day, pay attention to understanding this dynamic. Becoming cognizant of this relationship is another important move toward heightened internal self-awareness.

TUNE IN TO PHYSICAL SENSATIONS. Your physical sensations are linked to thoughts and feelings. They can tell you if you're in distress or at ease. For instance, a tight throat might be a sign you're feeling embarrassed, or relaxed hands might be a sign you're feeling calm. When strolling through the park to meet a friend, your footsteps might be light and quick, but when walking to a high-stakes meeting, your footsteps might be heavy. Just as Sophia did, as you go about your day, pay attention to your physical sensations to raise your internal self-awareness.

Let's combine thoughts, feelings, and physical sensations to see how they work together. We'll use this negative thought: *I need to come up with something to say in this meeting but I don't want to sound dumb.* This kind of self-imposed pressure and doubt may cause you to feel agitated, discouraged, and worried. When you tune in to your body, you might notice, for instance, that your shoulders are slumped, your jaw is tense, and your left eye is twitching. Combined, these sensations are likely to interfere with your ability to contribute to the meeting the way you want. No wonder you're having a hard time thinking of something to say! On the flip side, let's say you're in a different meeting and have a positive thought: *I love this project we're working on.* You might feel enthusiastic, passionate, and optimistic. When you pay attention to your body's sensations, you might notice a calm heartbeat, relaxed arms, and lightness in your chest. These examples show the interplay of thoughts, feelings, and physical sensations. Challenge yourself to pay attention to them and watch your self-awareness blossom.

Let's put all this together in a real-life example. Jennie, a former client of mine, works at a manufacturing facility, where she is vice president of projects and corporate planning. Exceptional at her job, Jennie is respected and well-liked. Despite that, she consistently procrastinated when it came to asking colleagues why particular projects were behind schedule and what could be done to get them back on track.

"I don't want to procrastinate," she told me. "But it feels like I'm carrying a sandbag on my shoulders. I hate confronting people."

Through our coaching sessions, Jennie learned to become familiar with her unhelpful thoughts, which included the following: *Oh, people are busy. I don't want to put more on their plate. I'm sure they know they need to get the project back up to speed. I don't want to bug them and put them under more pressure. I don't want to be difficult.*

As we explored her feelings about her own inaction—anxiety, helplessness, and frustration—we also discussed her physical sensations—tension in her head, tightness of her throat, and a heaviness in her shoulders. Jennie started to become more aware of the dynamic relationship among her thoughts, feelings, and physical sensations. As she paid more attention, she learned how to stop the negative thoughts. She also tuned in to her feelings and interpreted them. And when she felt physical discomfort, she breathed deeply to relax her body. Over time and with dedicated practice, her heightened internal self-awareness allowed her to overcome her fears and procrastination habits. What relief she felt! By equipping herself with this newfound self-awareness, Jennie now feels much more confident and at ease in her job. Let's explore some of the strategies Jennie used.

> **DEEP BREATHING.** Deep breathing brings you into a relaxed state, where you can think more clearly and see situations from a broader perspective. When you're relaxed, you're also better able to understand

your thoughts and feelings. Deep breathing also calms body sensations, moving you from physical distress to composure and relaxation.

MINDFULNESS. Focusing on the present moment helps you tune in to your thoughts, feelings, and physical sensations. Mindfulness can be practiced anytime and anywhere—while walking, brushing your teeth, sitting at a red light, or making your morning coffee. Pick an everyday activity and be exceedingly mindful when you do it. For example, when making coffee, pay close attention to all the sounds, aromas, and temperatures. Be keenly aware of the sound of the water as you pour it into the pot's reservoir and as it begins to bubble and boil. Pay close attention to the sound of the coffee as you pour it into your cup. Take in all of the various aromas, from the dry grounds to the liquid coffee. As you drink, pay attention to the temperature of the coffee and the cup you're holding, from the first sip to the last. Notice, too, the taste of every sip by taking in all the flavorful notes. The more mindful moments you can add throughout your day, the more self-aware you'll become.

MOVING AND STRETCHING. Move your body while simultaneously paying attention to how the movements feel. For example, as you walk from one place to the next, pay attention to your limbs and muscles, noticing what it feels like to move. Or, as you reach to pick up an object, pay attention to the sensation of reaching, grasping, and lifting. You can also stretch your hands over your head or reach them down to your toes while noticing how your body feels. Pay attention to each muscle, limb, and ligament. Or, as you walk from the carpet to a tiled floor, notice the sensations of your feet as they adjust from a soft surface to a hard one. While you do these movements, be mindful of your thoughts and feelings as well as the physical sensations. Also, notice how your body feels before and after moving and stretching.

JOURNALING. Writing down your thoughts, feelings, and physical sensations allows you to process them more fully, just like Sophia did. Journaling can help you see repetitive thoughts that may be holding you back or feelings that can cause you to spiral downward. Journaling can also help you connect physical sensations to your thoughts and feelings.

MEDITATION. Sitting in silence for a period of time helps you observe and understand yourself without judgement. Meditation helps you to be fully present in the moment so you can quiet your thoughts and tune in to your body. As described by Mindworks, meditation helps you let go of negative thoughts while promoting positive thinking. In addition to sitting quietly for a period of time, find small moments in your day when you can be in silence—like when your computer is booting up or you're waiting for the microwave to heat your lunch. Sprinkling in moments of silence during your regular activities gives you small respites without adding an activity to your to-do list.

These strategies can help you strengthen your internal self-awareness. I encourage you to try them on for size and come up with some of your own. Experiment and make a game of it to see which ones you enjoy the most. You'll be more likely to stick with activities you like.

Remember, self-awareness isn't a luxury; it's vital. As explored earlier in this chapter, research shows that self-aware leaders have a competitive advantage. If you want to stand out from the crowd, then mind your thoughts, assess your feelings, and tune in to your physical sensations. This will lead to more self-awareness. By doing so, you'll be on your way to becoming part of the 10 to 15 percent of people who are self-aware.

External Self-Awareness

Let's flip the coin over to look at external self-awareness, which is understanding how other people see you. People's perceptions of you may vary, but understanding them is a great way to develop self-awareness. It also helps you know if you're perceived the way you want to be. Do you see yourself in the same way other people do? Do you think you're coming across one way when it's actually another? One of the best ways to elevate your external self-awareness is by getting feedback.

Rachel is a chief ethics and compliance officer at a global pharmaceutical company. Over the years, she had risen through the ranks until she was leading the second-largest division in the organization.

The operational and financial portfolios she managed were impressive, as were the number of people reporting to her. By all accounts, Rachel had made it, weathering storms along the way with grace and determination. Despite her stellar reputation as a leader and her results-oriented track record, Rachel feared getting feedback from others. With everything she had been through professionally—all the corporate politics, tough decisions, and relentless pressures—you wouldn't think feedback would be so hard for her. But it was.

"I know it's irrational, and I wish I didn't feel this way," Rachel confided in me. "But it's a fear I've struggled with for years." She held herself to an exceptionally high standard, so any hint of criticism hit her hard. She didn't reject or dismiss the feedback; she just really took it to heart. As Rachel began practicing the internal and external self-awareness strategies she'd learned through our coaching sessions, she became more comfortable asking for feedback. Eventually, she welcomed it with open arms. There are two types of feedback beneficial to building external self-awareness: indirect and direct.

> **INDIRECT FEEDBACK.** Think about words or phrases you've heard said about you. Now, take out a piece of paper and jot them down. Keep the list handy so you can continue adding to it. You can also take your list to meetings to capture words said about you in real time. After a week or so, go back through the list and look for themes. For example, words such as *organized*, *prepared*, *methodical*, and *structured* have similar meaning. Likewise, *strategic*, *visionary*, and *future-oriented* can be categorized as a common theme, as can *creative*, *original*, and *imaginative*. By writing down the words you hear and grouping them

into themes, you'll collect indirect feedback about how other people see you.

Another kind of indirect feedback is other people's body language. Because communication is both verbal and nonverbal, body language offers important hints about how people feel about you. Do people seem relaxed around you? In meetings, do people shy away from sitting near you? When people see you, do they seem friendly or reserved? You can also pay attention to something called "mirroring." This is when your body language and that of another person's mimic each other—for instance, you're both leaning forward, have your arms crossed, or are resting your chin on one of your hands. Mirroring is a good sign that you have rapport. Interestingly, paying attention to someone's feet can also be a source of information. People usually point their feet in the direction they want to be. If you see someone's feet pointed toward you, that tends to be a favorable sign. On the flip side, feet pointed away from you may be a clue that the person is uncomfortable. Body language provides important clues that are worth considering.

DIRECT FEEDBACK. Direct feedback is asked for explicitly. This can be done by directly asking people for it or through a feedback tool such as a 360-degree assessment. In my experience, the higher you are in an organization, the more important it is to get direct feedback. Trouble is, the higher your position, the more reluctant other people are about giving feedback to you. This is something Rachel knew well and something we talked about in our coaching sessions. At her level, she knew she held a lot of power. If she wanted honest feedback, she'd have to make it as comfortable as possible for people. We explored how to go about this, and she took deliberate steps to create the right environment. First, she made it known to her team that she wanted their feedback. In both group settings and one-on-one meetings, she consistently asked, "How can I be a better leader for you?" and "What could I have done differently?" At first, she was discouraged and thought about giving up because people only gave vague responses that weren't useful. She persevered, though, and over time, people started opening up, giving her specific feedback that helped her become a more effective leader. I remember her telling me, with great enthusiasm, "I'm so happy I didn't give up. It took a while, but I'm so appreciative of the great feedback I'm getting." It was not only her consistency in asking for feedback but also her genuine receptivity that created an honest and safe environment for sharing. She listened with interest and curiosity, not judgement. She made it a point to gently lean forward, nod her head in understanding, and ask clarifying questions. She also took action on what she heard. Not only that, she took it a step further by closing the feedback loop; she circled back with people to let them know the specific actions she had taken based upon their feedback. Because of Rachel's efforts, people became comfortable giving her feedback and, in turn, her self-awareness grew.

Another strategy to get direct feedback is sharing a real-life mistake you've made. Admittedly, this takes courage. Most of us don't like to disclose mistakes, especially if we're in a leadership position. However, mistakes are a great way to learn and an opportunity to get feedback. Think of a mistake you recently made. It can be minor. Share the mistake with a trusted colleague. It's ideal if the person is someone you can count on to be truthful and candid. Tell them you want their honest feedback about what you could have done differently. You can ask, "What were my blind spots? What other steps could I have taken? What else could I have considered? Who else could I have involved?" Their answers can provide valuable insights about how other people see you, including their perceptions about your thinking, actions, and behaviors.

External feedback is the most robust when both direct and indirect feedback are combined. This combination paints a vivid picture that can help shape and strengthen your self-awareness. Jessica, vice president of philanthropy and planned giving at a university, understood this. Her boss, the senior vice president, was retiring in a few months, and Jessica had her eye on being promoted. She was savvy enough to know to use the upcoming months to her advantage, so she'd be well positioned for the promotion. And she knew it would be more powerful to engage in Collaborative Confidence. She approached Molly, a trusted colleague with whom she had a long-standing relationship, and shared the meaning of Collaborative Confidence: "I'm responsible for my own confidence, and I'm responsible for helping other women with theirs."

Molly's eyes lit up. She was immediately receptive and ready to practice Collaborative Confidence. Jessica's next step was to go on a self-awareness journey. First, she made a list of words she'd heard people use to describe her and then put them into themes that included thorough, trustworthy, dependable, humble, reserved, and cautious. She shared the list with Molly, who added *loyal* as another word. They talked further about the words, sharing stories that illustrated why Jessica was known for these traits. Jessica also paid attention to people's body language and realized that people were friendly but a bit reserved around her. She wondered if she could do something to change that. She and Molly talked about this and decided the next best step would be to ask for direct feedback. Jessica was scared, but with Molly's support, she courageously asked a handful of colleagues.

What she learned was eye-opening and confirmed what she was already picking up on through paying attention to indirect feedback. People told her that she was almost invisible. In meetings, she sat in the back of the room and rarely spoke up. They also said that when she led a project, she let other people take center stage while she came across more like a team member rather than someone who was in charge. And finally, people told her that she rarely shared her opinion unless asked and when she did, she hemmed and hawed, coming across as uncertain. For someone wanting a promotion to a senior role, she alarmingly learned that although people liked working with her and although she did a good job, they didn't see her as a leader. Yikes! The feedback hit her hard, and she felt discouraged. *How can I turn things around in just a few months?* she thought. But Jessica wasn't about to be stopped. Plus, she knew she had Molly's encouragement and support. After some sleepless nights, a few long bike rides, and several deep conversations with Molly, she took to heart everything she had learned and went into action mode. Jessica knew she could do the senior vice president job well. She just needed other people to see her potential. She and Molly brainstormed and came up with several ideas. In meetings, she started to sit in the front of the room. She made it a point to ask questions and give her opinions in definitive language. The first few times, her heart raced and she felt flushed. Over time, these physical sensations subsided. She stopped saying, "I'm not sure," and started using phrases that conveyed more confidence. At first, it was hard to keep such words from flittering out, but the more she deliberately omitted them, the more natural it became. She also used her body language to make people feel more at ease by initiating handshakes, mirroring them, and smiling more. In team meetings, she raised her prominence by taking charge of driving the agenda and setting clearer expectations. In the end, her efforts paid off, and she was promoted to senior vice president. Today, Jessica and Molly continue to practice Collaborative Confidence. Both have benefitted from their efforts and credit the reciprocal support, encouragement, and reassurance that is at the heart of Collaborative Confidence.

Remember what's at stake here. Developing greater self-awareness creates a key competitive advantage for leaders. Think of it as your own secret sauce. You'll be a more effective leader and a better person as a result. Remember the stories of Sophia, Yolanda, Jennie, Rachel, and Jessica. Let them help you see what's possible for you. Rely on Collaborative Confidence to support you on your path forward. Find another woman, like Jessica did, who can champion you and you her. Recall other benefits that self-awareness evokes including better strategic and financial performance, enhanced leadership effectiveness, and personal happiness. The beauty of self-awareness is that it's at your disposal 24/7, 365 days a year. You simply need to make an intentional decision to work on it—not just once or for a week, but for the long run. Think of it as a multiplier; the more you work on your self-awareness, the more it grows. It's like a bank account that never stops earning interest. Challenge yourself to be among the 10 to 15 percent of people who are self-aware. You'll soon enjoy the many professional and personal benefits of greater self-awareness.

Quiet Your Critics and Boost Your Champion

> *If I make a mistake, I'm going to get in a lot of trouble. All the fingers of blame will point at me, so I better triple-check all my i's are dotted and t's are crossed.*
>
> *If I don't take control and do it myself, it won't be done right.*
>
> *I don't have the experience I should by now. Other people are much more qualified than I am.*
>
> *If I speak up in meetings and say the wrong thing, I'll make a fool of myself and everyone will judge me.*

D oes any of this internal dialog sound familiar? Do you have your own version of these mean, discouraging, self-critical messages? What do you say to yourself about yourself? What makes this all the more crazy is that the horrible things we say about ourselves are things we'd never say to another person. We're all familiar with that pesky internal voice that constantly criticizes, belittles, and judges us. I know I am. This voice goes by many names: inner critic, judge, saboteur, gremlin, and superego, to name a few. Its job is to dish out a relentless barrage of negative self-talk inside your head. How exhausting!

The good news is that, through practice and discipline, you can quiet your inner critic and boost your inner champion. I had the great fortune to complete a coach-training program led by Shirzad Chamine, author of *Positive Intelligence: Why Only 20% of Teams and Individuals Achieve Their True Potential and How You Can Achieve Yours,* that focused on doing just that. It was extraordinary to get to know my own collection of saboteurs (the term Chamine uses) and understand their destructive impact. It was relieving to learn strategies to quiet them through various sage practices (the term he uses to describe your inner champion). While my own experience was eye-opening, it was all the more powerful to lead clients through this extraordinary work.

Jasmine, a former client who is a very experienced regional vice president of marketing for a national retail chain, doubted herself despite her impressive track record and title. She oversaw the marketing strategy for eight retail stores in a major metropolitan market. She was also a member of the company's executive steering committee. Yet, she constantly doubted herself, pushing herself to achieve more and more and never stopping to relax or pat herself on the back. Her focus was on achieving bigger and better results. She'd think to herself, *I have to be outstanding to prove myself. I must always be at the top of my game. I can only add value when I'm successful and other people see me that way.* On top of pushing herself hard to achieve, she constantly tried to make other people happy. She valued relationships and didn't want to let others down or hurt their feelings. In her relentless pursuit of achievement, she put the needs of other people ahead of her own. She feared rocking the boat, alienating people, and losing relationships. Because she wanted to be liked and fit in, she was almost always agreeable, even if she had a contrary point of view. As a result, she often felt resentful, worried, and stressed. She also second-guessed herself a lot, even questioning if she belonged on the executive steering committee.

During our coaching sessions, Jasmine learned how her saboteurs were hard at work. They were the source of her constant pressure, worry, and stress. In our coaching sessions, we explored simple yet powerful strategies to quiet them. Her consistent practice in a relatively short amount of time paid off, and the pressure, worry, and stress began to fade. Through continued practice, she kept her saboteurs at bay and strengthened her sage. She could think more clearly, be more resourceful, and feel more at ease. Along the way, Jasmine was surprised to discover she could still drive results without feeling stressed and anxious. She hadn't thought that was possible. She also found she could give contrary opinions without ruffling feathers or making people unhappy. This was another revelation.

The growth Jasmine experienced came from Positive Intelligence, the science and practice of developing mastery over your own mind so you can reach your full potential for happiness and success. Positive Intelligence was coined by Chamine and is based on his extensive research stemming from the fields of neuroscience, performance science, cognitive psychology, and positive psychology. His coach-training program allowed me to help many of my clients become familiar with their own saboteurs and take active steps, just like Jasmine did, to quiet them while bolstering their sage.

Whether you prefer to call it your inner critic, saboteur, gremlin, or something else, that pesky, negative voice that fills your head with criticism, doubt, and fear has some common characteristics. The voice tends to be automatic and persistent, like a broken record. It clouds your perception, decisions, and actions. It hampers your ambition and punishes you for even the smallest of mistakes. With such outlandish characteristics and devastating effects, why do we have inner critics? Neuroscience offers answers. The amygdalae are the parts of the brain primarily involved with processing emotions and memories. There are two amygdalae, one in each hemisphere of the brain. Either amygdala can be stimulated by emotions or a perceived threat. As John Hopkins explains in a blog post, "The amygdalae regulate emotion and memory and are associated with the brain's reward system, stress, and the 'fight or flight' response." As some of the oldest parts of the brain, one of the amygdalae's primary tasks is your survival. The amygdalae are also home to our inner critics—a whole committee of them. I know my inner critics can get quite chatty at times. In certain circumstances, one critic might take center stage over the others, but we all have more than one.

While juggling their committee of inner critics, female leaders often walk a tightrope. In our coaching sessions, my clients and I look for ways to ease this strenuous experience, but it's challenging. Leaders of all genders are expected to show traits such as ambition, confidence, independence, competence, and decisiveness. However, according to research by Dr. Anyi Ma, an assistant professor at Tulane University, those characteristics can label a woman as bossy unless balanced with warmth and approachability. Similarly, a 2018 *Harvard Business Review* article by Wei Zheng, Ronit Kark, and Alyson Meister found that women must be both warm and nice in addition to competent and tough. Likewise, Susan Fleming, a senior lecturer at Cornell, says, "A female leader is supposed to be strong and authoritative, know her stuff, hold her ground and speak her mind, but while doing that, she is simultaneously also supposed to come off as sweet, supportive, nice, communal, kind and gentle." What a tightrope! This precarious balancing act creates an environment in which inner critics can thrive.

And trying to calm a committee of inner critics while walking a tight-rope is no small feat.

What's the tightrope you balance on? What did you not say in a meeting because you were afraid of not saying it well or being labeled as bossy? What did you not take a stand on even though you knew it was the right thing to do? How often do your inner critics go over and over and over something you did, telling you that you didn't do it right or that you didn't come across in the right way? How fre-quently do you second-guess yourself—checking, double-checking, and triple-checking? Oh, and maybe even checking again.

Let's distinguish between learning from our mistakes and berat-ing ourselves. There's a big difference. We all make mistakes. They provide an opportunity to reflect and learn. When you take away an insight or lesson from a mistake and give yourself grace and forgive-ness to move on, that's healthy. When you relive the mistake and let your inner critics relentlessly admonish you, that's not healthy. That's where the work to discern the difference between the two comes in.

This is exactly why in my work with women leaders, I make it a priority to help them quiet their inner critics. Having your profes-sional life (not to mention your personal life) ruled by inner critics is exhausting and stressful. I've seen it hold back far too many talented women leaders. For example, Margaret, who works for a graphic de-sign business, was so concerned about not making mistakes that she took painstaking effort to guarantee her work was perfect, often re-sulting in working evenings and weekends. On top of that, she wanted to be the consummate team player, so she constantly lent a hand to others even at her own expense. She was walking a tightrope, and her inner critics were right there with her. Unfortunately, Margaret didn't take charge of her inner critics. Instead, she allowed them to rule over her and lived with their constant badgering to produce perfect work and be the consummate team player. Just imagine how life would improve for Margaret if she quieted her inner critics and put her inner champion in charge. What might be possible for her? Now, think about yourself. Imagine if your inner champion was in charge. How would it make walking that tightrope easier? How different might work feel? Think of all you could accomplish while feeling at ease.

The qualities of your inner champion are the opposite of those of your inner critics. Your inner champion makes you feel resilient, optimistic, and resourceful. Your thinking is clear, focused, and level-headed when your inner champion is in charge. You feel capable, confident, and authentic. You are your true, natural self. How refreshing! When my clients tap into their inner champion, they describe a sense of purpose, expansiveness, and lightness. They also talk about feeling grounded. That's because your inner champion reminds you of your intrinsic worth. With your inner champion in charge, you're able to see possibilities and move beyond your current circumstance. That's why it's important to do the work to empower your inner champion. With intention and regular practice, you can learn to quiet your inner critics and strengthen your inner champion, just like Jasmine did. In fact, by quieting your inner critics, you automatically awaken and strengthen your inner champion. Think of it like a seesaw: as one side goes down, the other automatically goes up.

My client Lauren found herself unsure how to handle some distressing events happening at work. She worked for an aerospace company as the associate vice president of quality control and assurance. There had been a lot of turmoil in her division, including turnover and complaints, which had led to several internal investigations. While Lauren hadn't been the focus of these investigations, they were all around her. She felt like a fish swimming in a bowl of dirty water. On top of that, her division head transferred a difficult employee into her department and wanted the person promoted. I'm sure you can imagine the stress this generated for Lauren. It was a perfect environment for her inner critics to take charge. They love feeding off stress, anxiety, and pressure. In our coaching sessions, we worked together to quiet her inner critics and bolster her inner champion. There are several ways to activate your inner champion, but in one particular session, we did a visualization. While breathing slowly with her eyes closed, I asked Lauren to hold her inner critics in one hand and her inner champion in the other. As the visualization continued, I asked her to release her inner critics by allowing their energy to float above her hand and dissipate. Then I asked her to allow her inner champion's energy to seep into her other hand and spread throughout her entire body. Afterward, she said simply doing the visualization made her feel more relaxed and in charge. But we didn't leave it there. We also worked together to come up with specific actions to keep her calm and levelheaded so her inner champion would remain in charge, even in stressful situations. She made the following changes: First, she blocked off her calendar so she could focus on her work without being interrupted. Second, she delegated a particular project to one of her direct reports. And third, she decided she would take deep breaths throughout the day, first in the morning while her computer boots up and then at the start of every meeting. She later told me these simple actions made her feel more focused, grounded, and self-assured— even in the midst of a tumultuous work environment. She felt her inner champion was becoming much stronger, and she could identify her inner critics more quickly and shoo them away with ease.

Let's turn back to neuroscience to understand how activating specific regions of your brain quiets your inner critics and strengthens your inner champion. Shifting attention away from negative thoughts and feelings to the physical sensations of your body, specifically your five senses, can help. When you pay attention to physical sensations, you activate the region of your brain associated with your inner champion. This allows you to think clearly and feel calm. With regular practice, you can create new neural pathways that strengthen your inner champion and diminish the power of your inner critics. Isn't it amazing to know that with only your five senses, you can change your brain? Similarly, research published in *Social Cognitive and Affective Neuroscience* shows that mindfulness and meditative practices correlate with structural changes in the brain. How empowering! You have the ability to rewire your brain to favor your inner champion.

Here are six simple and specific techniques to quiet the chatter of your inner critics and strengthen the nurturing, empowering voice of your inner champion.

> **CONTROLLED BREATHING.** Focusing on your breathing helps you relax, which immediately begins to quiet your inner critics and awaken your inner champion. According to research published in the *Journal of Neurophysiology*, slow, controlled, deep breathing activates the region of the brain that soothes thoughts and emotions, allowing you to feel calm. When you are calm, your inner champion is activated and in charge. Here are three deep-breathing exercises that can be done anywhere, anytime.
>
> > ○ **Abdominal Breathing.** Breathe deeply and slowly into your abdomen, inhaling and exhaling for a count of six. As you breathe, allow your lungs to fill up until you feel the sides of your body expand and contract. As

you practice abdominal breathing, pay close attention to all the physical sensations associated with inhaling deeply and exhaling completely. Take several deep, abdominal breaths for at least one minute and then return to regular breathing. Try a few rounds to get a deep experience.

○ **Box Breathing.** This is a time-honored breathing technique that's used by the Navy SEALs. You engage in a four-count rhythm of inhaling for four seconds, holding for four seconds, exhaling for four seconds, and holding for four seconds. Try several rounds of box breathing, then return to regular breathing. Remember to put all of your attention on the physical sensations of breathing as you practice this technique.

○ **Belly-Chest, Three-Part Breathing.** With this exercise, breathe deeply into your belly, pause, sip a bit more air into your chest, pause, and slowly exhale. Try at least three rounds, then return to normal breathing. Repeat three times, with focused attention on the physical sensations associated with this rhythmic breathing pattern.

SENSE OF TOUCH. Remember, when you pay close attention to any of your five senses, you activate the region of your brain associated with your inner champion. Here's how to use your sense of touch to awaken and strengthen your inner champion.

- ○ **Rub Your Fingers and Hands Together.** Gently and slowly rub your thumb and a finger together with careful attention. Notice the ridges of your fingerprints and all the sensations of gently rubbing your thumb and finger together. Continue doing this for about sixty seconds. With the same careful attention, put both your hands together as if you are about to pray. Then, gently slide the fingers of one hand all the way down to the base of the palm of the other. Continue this gentle sliding motion up and down as you allow the fingers and palms of each hand to glide against the other, moving back and forth, up and down. As you do this, for about sixty seconds, pay close attention to the physical sensations in your hands. Notice all the ridges, nooks, and crannies of each hand as they slide back and forth.

- ○ **Do Household Chores.** You can pay attention to your sense of touch when doing everyday household chores. Pick a specific chore (perhaps making your bed, folding the laundry, or washing the dishes), and as you do it, pay close attention to your sense of touch. Feel the texture, weight, temperature, and such as you do the chore. For instance, when making the bed, feel the weight and texture of the sheets, bedspread, and pillows. Notice the difference in how the fabrics feel. Take your time and allow yourself to become immersed in noticing your physical sensations as you make your bed.

o **Notice Your Clothing and Shoes.** Even what you're wearing offers an opportunity to explore your sense of touch. Take a moment to feel your clothes against your skin and your feet in your shoes. Notice sensations such as lightness, pressure, warmth, coolness, tightness, softness, etc. You can also adjust your clothing or shoes to compare your sense of touch before and after. For example, take one shoe off and leave one shoe on. Notice the different sensations in each of your feet.

MINDFUL EATING AND DRINKING. Many of us gobble down food quickly and miss the opportunity to fully experience the delightful taste, texture, and smell of what we're eating. Mindful eating allows you to savor the experience and activate your inner champion through the senses of smell and taste. Here are some mindful eating and drinking tips.

o **Pick a Meal.** Choose a particular meal to practice mindful eating. Take time to slowly chew your food. With each luxurious bite, notice all the sensations and flavors in your mouth. To make it all the more scrumptious, pay attention to the colors, textures, and aromas of your food, too. Pause before consuming each bite. Take your time so you can truly experience each and every delectable bite. Continue doing this for the duration of the meal.

○ **Consume a Beverage.** Pick a beverage and focus on all the physical sensations you experience as you drink it. Notice how your throat feels before and after taking a sip. Notice the sensation of the liquid in your mouth and as it goes down your throat. With a hot beverage, such as coffee, notice the temperature of the cup and the liquid, from the first sip to the last. Chances are you'll experience a difference.

NOTICE, NAME, AND REPLACE. Canadian psychologist Donald Hebb once famously said, "Cells that fire together, wire together." This means that the more you exercise a neural circuit in your brain, the stronger it becomes. Therefore, the repetitive thoughts of your inner critics keep getting stronger and stronger the more they come to mind unless you stop and replace them with positive ones. The moment you notice a thought from your inner critics, silence it and replace it with a positive one. For instance, if your inner critic says, *I'm not experienced* *enough to take on this job,* you can replace it with, *I'm resourceful and can get the support I need.*

PURPOSEFUL INVITATION. Pick a meeting or interaction and intentionally invite your inner champion to be in charge. Tell your inner critics they're not needed. Prepare by tuning in to how your inner champion thinks, acts, talks, moves, etc. You can also wear a favorite piece of clothing or jewelry that brings out your inner champion. Sometimes, I spray myself with a spritz of a special perfume I bought in Paris as a way to purposefully invite my inner champion to be present.

CREATE PERSONAS. Think about the personalities of your inner critics and inner champion. Then, create a persona for each, thinking of all the unique characteristics associated with them. You can use inspiration from a cartoon character, superhero, or famous person. Consider giving names to your inner critics and inner champion and drawing pictures of them. Keep the picture of your inner champion handy, so you can see her all the time.

Quieting your inner critics and strengthening your inner champion requires commitment and practice. It's a long-term commitment, but think about the payoff: less worry, stress, and anxiety and more resilience, resourcefulness, clearheaded thinking, and confidence. How glorious does that sound? As a female leader walking the tightrope of professional expectations, it's time to silence your inner critics and embolden your inner champion. Are you ready? If you sense any hesitation, perhaps that's your inner critics riling up. What a perfect opportunity to stop them in their tracks. I hope you've been inspired by the stories in this chapter and can see yourself taking action, just like Jasmine and Lauren. Start today with the simple and useful tools we've discussed. Bring your inner champion to center stage and kick your inner critics to the wayside. It will change your life.

Chapter 3

Establish Your Personal Core Values

When music publicist and manager Sarah Leung started her boutique public relations company, the French Toast Agency, in 2011, she knew it had to be a reflection of her true self. So, when asked, "What drives you to want to work with an artist?" in a July 2021 *Billboard* magazine interview, her answer came easily. "If I feel that an artist is passionate and has the drive, I don't care about the numbers. Of course, their talent, that's a no-brainer, but the two main factors are drive and authenticity."

Separately, Leung told me, "It's important that I do work that feels good to me and that I work with clients who are authentic. It's not about the money, it's about doing work that I'm passionate about in a way that matches my values. My values are part of who I am, and they are definitely part of French Toast." Leung made sure the core values she lives by (integrity, transparency, and authenticity) were woven into the fabric of her company's culture. These core values have helped Leung shape French Toast into a highly successful public relations agency in a very competitive market.

Her story is a reminder of the power of core values. When you focus on your core values, you spend time doing things that energize you. You attract the right people who are aligned with your core values, and this helps bring out the best in you. Core values are central to your happiness. In tough times, they sustain you. In good times, they help you thrive. Doing the work to define your core values and weaving them into the tapestry of your life also builds internal self-awareness.

In this chapter, we'll explore core values, providing you with tools to clarify and establish them. Let's look at research on company core values for guidance. As illustrated by the success of the French Toast Agency, an organization's core values can drive growth if they become part of the company's DNA. A company's core values are guideposts that steer decision-making, strategy, services, teamwork, and leadership. They also define a company and differentiate it from others.

According to author and management consultant Patrick Lencioni, "Core values are the deeply ingrained principles that guide all of a company's actions." He goes on to point out that "values can set a company apart from the competition by clarifying its identity and serving as a rallying point for employees." American Express concurs: "It takes more than a strong balance sheet for modern businesses to succeed. That's why it's important for companies to define a set of core values." Building on these thoughts, having strong, well-defined core values shifts a company from simply doing business to serving a noble cause or purpose. Research shows this has a positive effect on financial performance, customer and employee satisfaction, and growth. A 2020 Gallup case study reveals how a financial institution increased its net profit by a whopping 85 percent over a five-year period when it went through an organizational transformation process that started with clarifying its core values.

I'm sure, as a consumer, you can think of companies that have strong core values. You might be able to recall specific experiences you've had with a company that prove those values to be true. Perhaps organizations such as Ben and Jerry's, Nordstrom, and Patagonia come to mind.

Core Values Shape You

With this background knowledge on company core values, let's turn our attention to your values and how they shape your actions, emotions, and behaviors. PostivePsychology.com says it well:

> Values are tied in with ethics and morals; they guide our judgment and prepare us to choose actions according to their consequences. The human value system serves self-exploration, self-enhancement, and self-recognition. . . .

> Psychologists believe in the transformative power of values. Studies have shown that ethics and values can change our inner world and alter the way we perceive and react to stimuli. For example, a person who has regard for honesty will genuinely reflect the same in his actions. He is less likely to engage in behaviors such as lying, stealing, cheating, or using any unfair means to accomplish his goals.

> Whether personal, professional, social, or life-oriented, values make room for knowledge, wisdom, and heightened self-realization. They are

unique and individualized. We all choose different combinations of values in life, and these choices shape our actions and life decisions. Clarifying values is a great way to prioritize our life goals and understand what we truly desire to become.

Your values are shaped by many things: your upbringing, education, major life events and experiences, relationships, and professional life, to name a few. In particular, your childhood and family environment play a central role in the formation of your core values. They are central to who you are as a human being.

Your core values are as unique to you as your fingerprint. These essential beliefs are your internal guide and let you know when you're on or off track. They are a barometer of your daily choices, interactions, relationships, and career aspirations. They keep you grounded, even amid turmoil and adversity. When your core values are crystal clear and you live by them consistently, you have a greater sense of calm, balance, and authentic alignment.

Core values also influence your professional journey. In author Bill George's leadership classic *Discover Your True North*, he uses the analogy of a compass as he unpacks the topic of authentic leadership, of which values are a primary tenet. "Staying centered on your values is not easy," he writes. "You can easily drift off course as the temptations and pressures of the outside world pull you away from your moral center. But if you are centered through a high level of self-awareness, your compass can help you get back on track."

Sarah Leung faced such a pivotal moment at French Toast Agency, when the temptation of money and a prospective high-profile client tested her commitment to her corporate and personal values. She had recently lost a couple of clients, so landing this new lucrative client would have easily filled the financial void. Though the money and prestige were tempting, she told me, she realized the client wasn't a good fit for the core values that define her and her agency: integrity, transparency, and authenticity.

"As tempting as it was, I knew I couldn't do it. I wouldn't have felt good about myself, and no amount of money is worth that. I've worked too hard to risk what French Toast has come to be known for." By setting aside her inner critics, who tried to scare her about losing a potential client, and relying on her strong core values, she was able to confidently decline the opportunity.

"I have no regrets," she told me. Her decision was not by whim or chance; it was the result of her commitment to live and lead in alignment with clearly defined core values.

All too often, though, life gets busy, and people don't make the time to do this important inner work. What a mistake. If your core values are unclear or your commitment to them is wishy-washy, life feels chaotic and unfulfilled. No one wants to live that way, though far too many people do. Research shows that when people define and stick to a clear set of core values, it's easier to make decisions about their passions, career goals, and relationships. No matter where you are in your life and career, there's always an opportunity to define your core values. It can be a personal and professional game-changer, as Leung's story demonstrates.

In case you're not convinced, let me share one more story. Eva grew up in a loving family with parents with successful careers and two siblings. Her parents encouraged her to do well in school and get good grades, which she did. In her early childhood, she loved taking art classes and being involved in drama and singing. As the years went by, however, she allowed her artistic side to fade in favor of a more traditional path of academic achievement and a good, stable job. For many years, Eva worked in the marketing department of a large tele-communications company. Although she told herself and others that she was happy, deep down she knew she wasn't. While she performed well and contributed to her team, she left work each day feeling empty and unfulfilled. She recalls thinking, *There has to be something better out there for me.* As luck would have it, she stumbled upon a podcast about core values. Without exactly knowing why, it caught her attention, so she followed her intuitive impulse and listened to it. *Wow! How eye-opening. My work and values are at odds. No wonder I feel so off course and unhappy,* she thought. That first podcast led to similar ones popping up on her playlist. She started listening to them during her daily subway ride to and from work.

The stories she heard inspired her to begin the hard work to un-cover her personal core values. As this exploration unfolded, she real-ized her love of the arts had been buried. She came to understand she truly valued artistic expression and was longing to bring it back into her life. She began looking for a new job. As a result, Eva was able to leave her telecommunications job and put her marketing expertise to use at a prominent art museum. Now, at the new job, her internal compass is back on course, and she feels deeply fulfilled. What a joy it is to go to work every morning! She eagerly jumps into the day's activities, and time flies. The museum gives her full creative reign to shape marketing strategies and attract more patrons. Both the work and the environ-ment perfectly align with her core values. Walking through the muse-um's exhibition halls and soaking up the art feeds her soul. She makes it part of her everyday routine. The museum also encourages employees to take their public art classes, and Eva enthusiastically embraces every opportunity to sign up. Her house is filled with pottery, paintings, and sculptures she has made. In her personal life, Eva made changes, too, returning to her love of singing by joining a local community choir.

Eva's story is a reminder of the power of core values. Because she recognized her professional discontent and did something about it, she was able to transform her personal and professional life. She defined her core values and committed to live in alignment with them, giving her a renewed sense of direction and purpose. It also gave her the courage to make a life-changing career decision.

I hope Eva's and Sarah's stories inspire you to define your core values. It's time to take that step and integrate them into your life.

Tools to Identify Your Values

One way to get a solid understanding of your core values is to deconstruct experiences from your upbringing. This can reveal long-held values and why they're important to you. Begin by thinking back to your childhood. Consider the praise and rewards you received when you were young. Were you praised for high achievements like great grades and winning competitions? Or were you complimented for artistic expression and creative endeavors? Perhaps you were commended for sharing and helping others. Flip the coin over to consider what you were criticized for and how those experiences may have also shaped your values. Maybe you were criticized for not being orderly and organized or for speaking up too much and being too loud. You can also think about your overall family environment. Perhaps you grew up in a family with limited financial means, which fostered values associated with resourcefulness, prudence, or creativity.

Now, consider your life today and the values it reflects. Think about your job, family, and friends, as well as your favorite activities—cultural, physical, religious, political, social, etc. What do you spend your money on? This, too, says a lot about your values. Once you've completed this exploration of the past and present, you're in a good position to identify your core values. Perhaps you'll find that your values originating from childhood remain largely the same, as was the case for Eva. Or maybe you'll notice a shift in your values as you moved into your adult life.

Another way to clarify your core values is to think about peak experiences throughout your life. Peak experiences are those moments that last in your memory because of the personal meaning that comes from them. They may be your most uplifting and jubilant moments or deeply painful experiences that required courage and resolve. Peak experiences, whether joyful or painful, generate intense emotions, which are etched into powerful memories. For example, a peak experience that stands out for me is my first coaching class. When learning about this new profession, I felt like I was finally home.

Peak experiences, as described in *The Handbook of Humanistic Psychology*, tend to share three characteristics: they are fulfilling, significant, and spiritual. They are fulfilling because of the intense emotions they spark. They are significant because they increase self-awareness, which often leads to a turning point in life. They are spiritual because they bring about a feeling of oneness with the world. Another characteristic of peak experiences is that they cause contemplation; you find yourself thinking about them, dissecting them, and trying to make sense of them.

Take some quiet time to identify your peak experiences. Rather than thinking about your entire life, you may break it into ten-year segments. This can help you think through various experiences and identify the ones that were truly peak moments of vibrant joy or deep pain. Another way to segment your life is by your education. Look at your elementary school years, then middle school, high school, college, etc. Follow that with your first job and other milestones of your adult life. Vividly recall the significant moments in each segment of your life, including who you spent time with, what you were doing, where you were, and how you were feeling. As part of the exercise, pull these emotions into the present and allow them to wash over you—whether joy, excitement, pride, accomplishment, courage, resolve, agony, sorrow, etc. Finally, consider the core values that were at play during these peak experiences. Ask what they have in common and which themes stand out. In Eva's case, her peak experiences shared her core values of stability, independence, community, and uniqueness, in addition to artistic expression.

Identifying people you admire is another way to clarify your core values. Consider friends, family members, famous people, and historic figures. Get out a pen and paper and make two columns. In one, list the people you most admire. In the other column, write down the specific qualities you admire about them. After your list is complete, go back and circle qualities that appear more than once. Then look for qualities that have similar meaning so you can identify themes. For instance, qualities such as optimism, cheerfulness, and happiness have similar meanings, as do adventurousness, boldness, risk-taking, and thrill seeking. Once you've grouped the qualities by theme, step back to figure out how they line up with the true essence of who you are. Which qualities resonate? This exercise, along with others, helped Eva shape her core values, and it can do the same for you.

When you establish your core values and weave them into your life, everything changes for the better. Even when life throws you a curveball, your core values will envelop you, giving you a sense of courage and resolve. Leaders and companies committed to clear core values reap many benefits. People with strong core values make better decisions and choices. They engage in more fulfilling, authentic, and purposeful activities and relationships. They live the life they were born to live. This is powerful work, so make it a priority. Take the time to deconstruct experiences from your childhood, tease out your peak experiences, and identify the people you admire. Establish your core values and commit to living in alignment with them. Like Sarah and Eva, the beautifully woven tapestry you create by doing this important work will yield life-changing benefits and enrich the way you live, work, and lead.

Chapter 4

Leverage Your Strengths

A ccording to Gallup, people who use their strengths every day are six times more likely to be engaged at work, six times as likely to strongly agree they get to do what they do best, and three times as likely to say they have an excellent quality of life. A 2020 Gallup report also discusses the detrimental impacts of disengaged employees who don't regularly use their strengths. Gallup breaks this group into two categories: actively disengaged and not engaged. Actively disengaged employees are those who have miserable work experiences and spread their unhappiness to colleagues. According to Gallup, they represent approximately 14 percent of the workforce. Not engaged employees are "psychologically unattached to their work and company" and represent 54 percent of workers. While this group shows up to work and puts in their time, they lack energy and passion, causing them to contribute minimal effort. Gallup goes on to say such employees are "also on the lookout for better employment opportunities and will quickly leave their company for a slightly better offer."

As you look at this research, where do you see yourself? Are you among those who use their strengths every day, feeling engaged, doing what you do best, and enjoying an excellent quality of life? Or are you on the other side of the equation, among the actively disengaged or not engaged, not passionate or psychologically attached to your job?

Perhaps it's not surprising that strengths-based organizations—filled with engaged and productive people—perform better. Another Gallup study finds that strength-based development leads to:

- 10 to 19 percent increased sales,
- 14 to 29 percent increased profits,
- 3 to 7 percent higher customer engagement,
- and 9 to 15 percent increased employee engagement.

This research also has big implications for individuals. There's an undeniable connection between regularly using your strengths and feeling engaged at work and happy in life. However, when your strengths aren't tightly woven into the fabric of your job, your sense of engagement can become frayed and you risk becoming disengaged. I can relate. Back in my HR days, I yearned to use my strengths at work. But since those opportunities didn't exist, I left work most days feeling depleted and discouraged. If that's where you are right now, don't worry, there is a way out. It begins with finding your strengths and putting them to use.

Being in a Strengths Deficit

It's one thing to recognize your strengths, it's a whole different ball game to get to use them. How often do you get to use your strengths at work? Often? Infrequently? Somewhere in between? Do you feel engaged in your work? Are you enthusiastic, eager, and passionate? Do you care about your job and your organization? Do you work for more than just a paycheck?

Of course, it's not realistic to expect to use your strengths all the time at work. We all have tasks we prefer not to do. That's normal. We simply have to find a way to get the work done. Sometimes it means hunkering down and completing the job or delegating it if you're able. In my experience with clients, if the greater portion of their work plays to their strengths, then they feel engaged. It's when the balance is tipped in the other direction that my clients feel unengaged.

As discussed by James Harter and Amy Adkins in a 2020 *Harvard Business Review* article, when people are engaged, they are "involved in, enthusiastic about and committed to their work and workplace." When they're not engaged, their tank is empty and they feel "indifferent, sleepwalking through their workday without regard for their performance or their organization's performance." Is this you? I can recall periods in my work life when I felt like that. While I showed up with an intellectual desire do well and make a difference, my heart simply wasn't in it. I was dragged down by overwhelming feelings of sluggishness and indifference because the work didn't cultivate or capitalize on my strengths. Even though I tried to make the best of the situation and amp myself up, it just wasn't enough. I couldn't convince myself that my job was satisfying. My tank was empty. If your tank is empty and you're sleepwalking through work, it's time to turn things around. It's time to discover and start using your strengths, fill up your tank, and refuel your happiness and well-being.

As a human resources senior director at a major metropolitan hospital, Katherine was among the group of not engaged employees. She showed up to work every day but often with an empty tank. While she tried to do a good job, meet her boss's expectations, and contribute to her team's success, she was running on fumes. There were some aspects of her job that energized her, but the vast majority of her work felt draining and uninteresting. Much of her day revolved around analytical reporting and evaluating metrics associated with hiring rates, turnover trends, employee training, and staff performance. Intellectually, she knew her work was important to both the strategic direction of the human resources department and the entire hospital. Emotionally, though, her workdays were draining. Each evening, she went home to her family tired and dreading having to do it all over again the next day. She knew something had to change, but she was torn. On the one hand, she deeply believed in the hospital's mission and the community it served. She was impressed with its extraordinary patient care and proud to work for a hospital with such a stellar reputation. She had also been with the hospital for many years and had formed close, enjoyable relationships with many colleagues. What Katherine didn't realize at the time was that her job rarely allowed her to tap into her strengths.

Strengths Versus Skills

It's important to understand that strengths and skills are not the same. Skills are learned through repetition and practice and are used to accomplish specific activities. A skill could be an activity you learn when you start a new role or as your responsibilities increase. If you don't practice a skill, your ability to execute that skill may become rusty over time. For example, some people are gifted when it comes to learning languages. For me, learning a language is a skill, not a strength. When I studied French and used it while vacationing in France, I got by pretty well. But when I stopped speaking French, I quickly lost any gains I had made.

In the classic leadership book *Now, Discover Your Strengths*, authors Marcus Buckingham and Donald O. Clifton point out that skills will help you perform but not excel. The authors offer the example of being a public speaker. While you may practice and become an effective public speaker, you won't excel if it's not a strength. TMBC, a strengths-based talent-development consulting firm, describes a strength as "an activity that strengthens you. It draws you in, it makes time fly by while you're doing it, and it makes you feel strong." TMBC goes on to point out that people look forward to using their strengths. "It's an activity that leaves you feeling energized, rather than depleted." Let's also look at a description from Alex Linley, founding director of the Centre of Applied Positive Psychology, who says "a strength is a pre-existing capacity for a particular way of behaving, thinking, or feeling that is authentic and energizing to [you] and enables optimal functioning, development and performance." In other words, when you get to do what you do best, you *feel* your best. As described by *Positive Psychology*, strengths generate common thoughts such as the following: *I can't wait to start. This is fun. I could do this forever.* Feelings that often bubble up around strengths include passion, motivation, and enthusiasm. To summarize, the characteristics that define strengths include the following:

- You are able to perform with near perfection.
- You don't notice the passage of time.
- You are drawn toward activities that use your strengths.
- You feel energized, authentic, happy, connected, and productive.
- Your strengths are essential to who you are.

Before Katherine found her strengths, she managed to perform relatively well but at a huge cost. She woke up most days dreading work and slogged through the day. Her thoughts about her job included, *This work is hard and tedious.* She frequently felt exhausted, stressed, and worried. Physically, she experienced tension in her shoulders and neck. She knew her analysis had to be perfect—the hospital was depending on it—so she double- and triple-checked her work. She was self-aware enough to realize that crunching hard-core analytical data wasn't one of her strengths, so she put pressure on herself to get it right. She would soon learn that these were warning signals that she was not using her strengths. Her stressful work environment became rich soil for the chatter of her inner critics to grow and intensify. It comes as no surprise that the combination of her depleting work and self-imposed pressure caused mistakes to be made, which only made her job all the more grueling and her inner critics even chattier.

Identify Your Strengths

By now, hopefully you're motivated to identify your strengths. It's time to find your strengths so they can become part of your job. There are several ways to go about this, including choosing energizing activities, listening to good managers, and identifying your best days at work. Let's explore all of these.

CHOOSE ENERGIZING ACTIVITIES

How do you find your strengths and identify your weaknesses? I ask my clients to look at their current job and keep track of their activities for about a week or so. I encourage them to pay attention to specific activities that are energizing or depleting and record them in a notebook under one of four columns: Column one is energizing work activities. Column two captures the feelings associated with performing those activities.

Column three lists depleting work activities. Column four documents the feelings associated with performing those activities. Some of my clients get creative and put a plus sign or a green light above the energizing activities and a minus sign or a red light above the depleting activities. By the end of the week, the energizing column begins to reveal the client's strengths, while the depleting column starts to expose their weaknesses.

This is exactly what Katherine did. Her depleting column included responsibilities such as comparing hiring and turnover metrics per quarter and per year, evaluating a new software system for analytical reporting, reviewing the existing software system to ensure data integrity and security, and updating processes to improve data reporting efficiencies. The feelings she experienced included being tense, weary, sad, and worn-out. Her energizing activities column included writing narratives so the numbers tell a story, meeting with department heads to translate analytical data and metrics into understandable terms, and serving on a cross-functional strategic communications team. When doing these activities, Katherine felt energized, productive, and motivated. She was surprised to see that the majority—about 70 percent—of her forty-hour workweek was spent performing tasks that depleted her. No wonder she was worn-out! This exercise raised her self-awareness and was the first piece of tangible evidence she needed to make a change at work.

LISTEN TO GOOD MANAGERS

Sometimes other people see your strengths before you recognize them yourself. This was the case for Emily. Over the years, Emily rose through the ranks of a national bank to become the chief strategy officer. She admits that early in her career she was rather oblivious of her strengths, concentrating more on her performance and establishing good work relationships. But there were some key moments that helped her identify two of her strengths: influence and strategy. She noticed her boss often pointed out her natural ability to influence other people. On more than one occasion, he told her she had a real knack for rallying people around ideas and influencing them to take action.

These comments helped her see influence as one of her strengths. Her boss also pointed out her ability to be strategic. He complimented her for frequently seeing the big picture, analyzing variables, combining ideas, and anticipating outcomes. He also noted these natural strategic abilities in her annual performance reviews. Because of her boss's comments and encouragement, Emily became more self-aware and was able to recognize her strengths. Fortunately, Emily worked for a boss who drew attention to her strengths and, even better, gave her work assignments that capitalized on them. As she moved into higher roles at the bank, Emily continued using and refining her strengths. She attributes much of her success to those early years, when her first boss made it a point to acknowledge her strengths and give her assignments that leveraged them. He planted the original seeds that she cultivated over time, blossoming into a successful career. Wouldn't it be great if we all had a boss like Emily's?

Emily's story highlights the important role managers play when it comes to identifying and nurturing strengths. "The best way for employers to maximize employees' strengths," Gallup confirms, "is through their managers." Gallup goes on to point out, "When employees know and use their strengths, they are more engaged, perform better and are less likely to leave their company." Managers play a pivotal role because once they spot an employee's strengths, they can maximize opportunities for that employee to use their strengths through job responsibilities, stretch assignments, or special projects. Both the organization and employee benefit. "When employees feel that their company cares and encourages them to make the most of their strengths," Gallup continues, "they are more likely to respond with increased discretionary effort, a stronger work ethic, and more enthusiasm and commitment." *Positive Psychology* endorses this idea, stating that employees who apply their strengths at work are more effective, efficient, and satisfied.

YOUR BEST DAY AT WORK

Good managers, like Emily's, are well aware of the role they play in developing an employee's strengths. They make it a point to look for ways to cultivate and leverage their employees' strengths. A *Harvard Business Review* article by Marcus Buckingham, "What Great Managers Do," puts it this way: "There is one quality that sets truly great managers apart from the rest. They discover what is unique about each person and then capitalize on it." One way to identify an employee's strengths is to ask them a simple yet revealing question: "What was the best day at work you've had in the past three months?" This question helps reveal two important things. First, it reveals the kind of work an employee finds intrinsically satisfying, that is, the assignments, responsibilities, and tasks they genuinely enjoy and find motivating. Second, by digging below the surface, it's possible to learn *why* the work is motivating. For instance, if the best day an employee had at work was when their product development team recommended a new gadget, there's an opportunity to dig further to find out why. Was it because the employee loves working on a synergistic team? Was it because the employee gets a thrill out of beating the competition? Was it because the employee was involved in solving a complex problem? If you're a leader, make it a regular practice to ask your employees, "What was the best day at work you've had in the past three months?" Then, spend time unpacking the answer with more questions to go deeper to reveal their strengths. Once your employees' strengths have been identified, find ways to capitalize on them though assignments and other job-related opportunities.

If you work with other women, this same question—"What was the best day at work you've had in the past three months?"—offers a great opportunity to practice Collaborative Confidence. As you may recall, Collaborative Confidence means you're responsible for your own confidence and helping other women with theirs. In the case of strengths, you can help another woman identify her strengths while she does the same for you. This can be done regardless of whether you're her boss or not. You can work with a trusted colleague or friend to identify and nurture each other's strengths.

I recall a time when I felt shaky about my expertise and was unsure if I should pursue an opportunity. I reached out to a friend, and together we engaged in Collaborative Confidence, as we had on many other occasions. She helped me see strengths in myself that I was having difficulty recognizing. What a boost our conversation was! And what an important reminder to me about strengths of mine that I may not always recognize.

You can also practice Collaborative Confidence with a small group to unearth your strengths. As a group, you can help identify, illuminate, and nourish one another's strengths and build happier, more productive, and more successful careers.

Now, it's time to take the same question—"What was the best day at work you've had in the past three months?"—and turn it inward by asking it to yourself. If one particular day doesn't jump out, take the time to reflect on various work experiences from the past three months. Notice what bubbles up that was energizing, motivating, and made you feel like you were at the top of your game. Think, too, about which of your core values were involved and how they intertwined with your strengths. Beyond a single day, consider commonalities among your best days. What themes stand out? What common threads are woven through these experiences? What patterns emerge? What strengths do these experiences unveil?

When Katherine, our human resources senior director, asked herself this question, she recalled a day when she had met with a division head to discuss hiring and retention metrics. The conversation went much deeper than numbers. Katherine was able to dive into, uncover, and discuss the meaning and implications behind the numbers. Katherine's insights helped the division head get a clearer and broader picture of his troubling situation. By peeling back the layers, Katherine saw patterns and connections that revealed the root causes of the division head's staffing problems. She was thrilled by the discussion, enjoying the deeper analysis and being a valued advisor to the division head. She realized how energizing it felt to break down challenges into smaller parts, solve problems collaboratively, and offer advice that could lead to better outcomes. She felt a sense of ease, enthusiasm, and fulfillment. "Your insight and advice are helping me see solutions to combat the hiring and retention problems we've been having," she remembers the division head saying. What a great compliment!

Ultimately, Katherine realized that activities that played to her strengths included interpreting analytical data into understandable terms, writing narrative descriptions to explain data and metrics, collaborating with others to solve problems, and acting as an advisor. Equipped with this insight, she had a revelation that hit her like a lightning bolt one evening as she was preparing dinner: her current job responsibilities didn't play to her strengths! Her work was about number crunching, data security, and updating internal processes. No wonder she felt depleted. The more she thought about it, the more she realized her strengths and core values—achievement, collaboration, and resourcefulness—were not meaningfully represented in her work. By the time she went to bed, her head was swimming, causing a very restless night of sleep. The next morning before leaving for work, she texted her friend and colleague Lynne, asking if they could meet over lunch. At a patio table outside the cafeteria, Katherine shared her revelation. She noticed Lynne nodding in agreement.

"I've always noticed those strengths in you," Lynne told Katherine. "You love making numbers and data understandable for other people. I don't know anyone who does it better than you."

Katherine was relieved to get Lynne's validation. With crystal clear self-awareness, determination, and Lynne's encouragement, she began looking for a better job at the hospital. She thoroughly reviewed the hospital's job postings and relied on her strong internal network of trusted colleagues for help. She confided in a handful of people that while she intended to stay at the hospital, she was looking for a different job that played to her strengths and honored her values.

Within a few months, a position as a senior healthcare writer opened up, and Katherine got the job. It's a perfect match with her strengths and values. She now writes educational and research materials as well as the outcomes of clinical findings. She also updates research documents and communicates the findings to the hospital's medical team. She regularly collaborates with colleagues to analyze and document how to use equipment, technology, and medical devices to treat patients compassionately and effectively. Every day, her strengths are put to use. Her workday flies by, fueled by enthusiasm, happiness, and productivity. She is energized. Katherine now considers herself among those who are fully engaged at work. She comes home at night feeling motivated, energized, and looking forward to going back to work the next day.

Identifying your strengths is the starting point to unlocking enthusiasm and fulfillment at work. Before you can truly leverage your strengths and weave them into your job, you first have to identify them. By now, hopefully you're motivated to find your strengths and will capitalize on the strategies you've learned in this chapter.

Manage Your Weaknesses

We've talked a lot about strengths, so you might be wondering where weaknesses come into play. We all have them, and they shouldn't be ignored. Gallup defines weaknesses as "anything that gets in the way of your success." Their advice is not to ignore your weaknesses but to become aware of, take responsibility for, and use your strengths to manage them. Let's take a closer look at these three steps in further detail.

> **STEP 1: IDENTIFY YOUR WEAKNESSES.** External feedback is a great way to understand your weaknesses. You can directly ask for it or think about feedback you've already received—like from performance reviews or one-on-one conversations with your manager.
>
> Simone was a rising star at a biotech firm where she was a senior director of laboratory research. She had her sights set on moving up and didn't want anything to slow her down. By reading books and listening to podcasts about strengths, she knew becoming aware of her weaknesses was important. She pursued external feedback by asking her manager to help identify her weaknesses. She also looked back over several of her past performance reviews as well as a 360-degree assessment from the previous year. Looking at these as a whole, she noticed a theme: she could sometimes come across as too commanding or opinionated, leaving little room for discussion. She also discovered she needed to spend more time on

the professional development of her team; she had been lax about challenging, growing, and stretching their expertise.

STEP 2: TAKE RESPONSIBILITY FOR YOUR WEAKNESSES. There's no shame in admitting your weaknesses. Having educated herself on her strengths, Simone was ready to take responsibility for her weaknesses. She did her best to objectively think about the external feedback she had gathered. It should also be noted that her inner critics tried to persuade her not to take responsibility but instead blame others or circumstances for her shortcomings. Fortunately, she was able to stop her critics' chatter by using several of the techniques explored in chapter 2, including box breathing, gently rubbing her fingers together, and extending purposeful invitations to her inner champion. As she continued to think about the external feedback she had collected, she put herself in other people's shoes. This helped her see things from their perspectives and understand why she sometimes came across as too commanding and needed to focus on developing her team members' strengths and expertise.

STEP 3: MANAGE YOUR WEAKNESSES. Look at your strengths and consider how to use them to mitigate your weaknesses. Gallup offers the following as examples of questions you can ask when you are considering how to manage your weaknesses:

- How can you use your competitive nature to be a better listener?
- How can you use your relationship-building strengths to improve the quality of execution?
- How can you use your analytical-thinking strengths to influence others?

This is exactly what Simone did by asking, *How can I use my strength as a learner to be more receptive to other people's ideas?* In response, Simone decided to be genuinely curious about other people's opinions before giving her own. She made it a point to ask questions and patiently peel back the layers of other people's perspectives so she could learn from them. She realized how much she enjoyed the process of learning what others thought and felt. She found that this new perspective influenced, and sometimes softened, her point of view, which made her less commanding. She also asked, *How can I use my strength of achievement to grow and develop my team?* She decided to focus on the current strengths and experience of her staff and worked with them to identify how they wanted to grow professionally. It was exciting to see her team gain more experience and collectively achieve more than they had before.

Simone was already a rising star, but because she invested in her strengths and managed her weaknesses, her upward trajectory at the biotech firm continued. Not too long after, she was promoted to vice president of laboratory research. The cherry on top is that because she used her strength of achievement to bolster her team and helped them grow their own strengths and expertise, several of her team members were promoted at the same time. It was definitely a win-win!

Consider Leaving

You may have noticed that Katherine, Emily, and Simone all stayed with their employers. This is consistent with Gallup's research that employees who use their strengths are 15 percent less likely to quit their jobs. But maybe for you, staying with your employer is not the right option. You may be in a job that doesn't cultivate your strengths. And you may not have the support from your manager to nurture them. If this is the case, it may be time to look for a job elsewhere.

Before taking such a step, it may be worth talking with your boss. You don't have to divulge that you are considering leaving. Instead, reference your strengths and ask how you might use them in your current position. Explore possible ways to infuse more of them into your current job. You might consider sharing some of Gallup's strengths-based research about the benefits both employers and employees enjoy when strengths are part of the everyday work experience.

Preparation for this meeting is key. Make sure you clearly identify your strengths and weaknesses and compare them to the requirements of your job. Prepare talking points about how your strengths can be used in new or different ways. Come prepared with examples you and your boss can discuss. Be sure to think beyond your job description by considering special projects or committees where your strengths can be used. In the spirit of Collaborative Confidence, talk with a trusted female friend to help you prepare for the conversation. She'll likely see strengths in you that you don't see in yourself and be able to suggest how you can apply them at work. You can also role-play the conversation you plan to have with your boss. This way, you'll feel prepared and relaxed—and you'll know you have a supporter who is cheering you on behind the scenes.

If you do decide to look for a job elsewhere, keep your strengths in mind during your job search. Don't compromise and take another job just to escape your current work situation. Look for jobs and organizations where you are confident your strengths will be used. Do your research and assess the company culture carefully during the interview process. This way, you'll get a good idea if it's an environment where your strengths will be nurtured.

Uncovering your strengths and regularly using them at work makes you feel happy, motivated, and productive. I hope you have been inspired by the stories of Katherine, Emily, and Simone and will start your own strengths-based quest. Remember, what was possible for them is possible for you, too. When your self-awareness, inner champion, core values, and strengths are woven together, they represent the Activate pillar of Collaborative Confidence. The more you purposely weave these threads together, the more you'll know yourself and what you want out of work and life. You'll have what you need to create a beautiful tapestry that is unique to you.

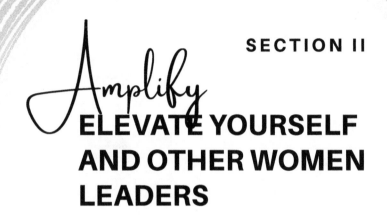

Amplify
ELEVATE YOURSELF AND OTHER WOMEN LEADERS

Women who make their presence and contributions known position themselves as strong, capable leaders. When you do this, it raises your visibility and sets you apart from the crowd. When you amplify the voices and contributions of other women, you truly epitomize the essence of Collaborative Confidence.

Chapter 5

Strengthen Your Executive Presence

The 2021 *Fortune* 500 list broke an important threshold: a record number of companies—forty-one, to be exact—were led by female CEOs. That was up by four from 2020. Not only that, for the first time, the list included two Black women—Roz Brewer of Walgreens Boots Alliance and Thasunda Brown Duckett of TIAA. Another female CEO, Karen Lynch of CVS, made history as the highest-ranking woman ever on *Fortune*'s list, positioned at number four. While this news is encouraging, it still means that only 8 percent of America's top companies are being led by women. That's pretty dismal. For many complex and systematic reasons, the playing field is not level for female leaders who aspire to reach the C-suite. And it's even tougher for women of color, as illustrated by *Fortune*'s numbers.

The challenges women face are compounded by workplace expectations. A *Harvard Review Business* article by Margarita Mayo describes research by her and her colleagues demonstrating the complex medley of characteristics required of female—but not male—leaders. As Mayo puts it, "Our study . . . shows that men are seen as confident if they are seen as competent, but women are seen as confident only if they come across as both competent and warm." Not only do women face such barriers as the glass ceiling (as illustrated by the *Fortune* 500 list), but they are held to a different behavioral threshold than men. Surely, their upward trajectory is impacted by this.

While companies need to make significant systematic changes to course correct such barriers, one strategy individual women can take is to focus on their executive presence. Organizational, systematic changes take time, but you don't have to wait. Take the reins now by building and amplifying your executive presence.

Although not clear-cut by definition, executive presence is something all effective leaders must master. A survey described in *Forbes* of more than four hundred CEOs, C-suite leaders, and executives found that 78 percent believe that a lack of executive presence can hold back a career. You can think of executive presence like the "it" factor of leadership—you know it when you see it. Perhaps you've been around someone and thought, *That person just seems to have "it."* *They're impressive.* Even after the person leaves the room, their presence, influence, and energy remain.

Tasha became one of those people as a result of her hard work on executive presence. To get from where she was to where she wanted to be, Tasha had to first learn to appreciate the power of executive presence and then learn the skills necessary to master it. After getting an undergraduate degree in entertainment management, she started her career as a production coordinator at one of the large Los Angeles entertainment studios. She loved the fast-paced, creative environment where she handled multiple projects at once. Over the years, she continued to thrive, eventually becoming executive vice president of North American media strategy. She found fulfillment, purpose, and passion as she advanced through the ranks. Through her experiences, Tasha realized that great leaders bring more to the table than just technical skills and intellectual horsepower. They present and carry themselves in a way that conveys credibility and influence. From observing other leaders, talking with her bosses, and reading business books, Tasha came to understand the power and impact of executive presence. As her career blossomed, she remained committed to cultivating her executive presence because she understood its value, knowing it would accelerate her career's forward motion—which is exactly what it did.

Executive presence begins with you. The foundation for executive presence is self-awareness, which we discussed in the Activate pillar section of this book. Before you can master executive presence, you must know how to gather and assess internal and external feedback. You must be able to quiet your inner critics and bolster your inner champion, as well as acknowledge your core values and recognize your strengths. Once you've developed a strong sense of self-understanding, you're ready to develop your executive presence. In my experience, executive presence comprises three overarching characteristics: authentically showing up, confidently presenting yourself, and genuinely connecting with others. As a female leader, it's my belief that the blending of these characteristics allows you to be seen as warm and competent, and therefore confident, as discussed by Mayo in her *Harvard Business Review* article. You can amplify and raise the visibility of your unique leadership style by weaving these into your day-to-day work relationships and interactions.

Authentically Showing Up

Tasha has always been a keen observer. Even in the early days of her career, noticing how the people around her behaved and interacted came naturally. She also has a real knack for building strong, trusting work relationships. Because of this natural talent, she worked well with her various bosses in an environment of open communication and respect. It was not unusual for her to talk about her career aspirations with her various bosses. Her curious, personal observations of other people and career-oriented conversations with her bosses began to shed light on the importance of executive presence.

Tasha learned that leaders with strong executive presence hold a set of personal characteristics that allow them to authentically show up. They are self-aware, trust their inner champion, rely on their strengths, and lead by their core values. With this knowledge, and her desire to continue moving up in the organization, Tasha committed to developing these characteristics and began weaving them into her leadership style. She requested regular feedback from her bosses, colleagues, and peers. She worked to quiet her inner critics and bolster her inner champion through box breathing and the notice-name-replace technique. She carved out time to establish her core values through deconstructing childhood experiences and identifying peak experiences. And she identified her strengths by tracking activities that energized her or depleted her. Through all of this, Tasha's self-awareness grew exponentially, allowing her to authentically show up anywhere, in any room, with any group of people. She also learned the following characteristics of authentically showing up:

> **BEING FULLY PRESENT.** Have you ever been around someone when it was obvious their mind was somewhere else? Even if they were sitting at the conference room table right across from you and looking straight at you, it was clear their attention was somewhere else. When someone is not present, others in the room don't feel valued or important. To

be fully present, you must be conscious of where you are, what you're doing, and who you are with. You're not distracted by any internal or external chatter— like worrying about your next meeting or your to-do list. Your phone is not on the table, distracting you. You are focused on the other people, making them feel valued, heard, and acknowledged.

If you struggle to be fully present, you can use something I call the ABC technique. The letter A means *arrive*, B stands for *breathe*, and C means *connect*. A reminds you of where you are and prompts you to commit to being present. You're not thinking about your next meeting, phone call, or commute home. You have arrived, and this is where you are, so be present. B reminds you to do just that—breathe. Take a few long, deep breaths to settle into the present moment. C reminds you to acknowledge the other people around you. Take a moment to scan your surroundings, make eye contact with other people, and nod or smile at them.

Being present also means you are aware of your thoughts, feelings, and physical sensations, as we discussed in chapter 1. Tune in to your thoughts and manage them until you are fully present. Notice whether your feelings are helping or hindering you from actively and fully participating in the moment you're in. If they're hindering you, find another feeling that helps you shift into the present. Notice your physical sensations to see if they're helping or distracting you. If they're distracting, do something to soothe them such as shift in your chair, stretch, or change positions. You can also use your sense of touch, such as gently rubbing your fingers and hands together (as discussed in chapter 2), to help you become more present.

BRINGING THE RIGHT PERSONAL ENERGY.
Everyone's personal energy affects the atmosphere
of a room or interaction. Have you been in a meeting where the person running it was harried and
stressed? Maybe they were flustered, ill-prepared, or
moved through the discussion so erratically it was
hard to follow their ideas. Conversely, have you been
in a meeting where the person leading it was calm,
collected, confident, and clear? Even if it was in the
wake of a crisis, the person was composed and ex-
uded a calming energy. Or what about those who
intimidate and exert too much authority? How does
their energy impact you and others? Compare those
feelings to ones you've had around leaders who are
open, are collaborative, and listen well. How does
their energy impact you? Positively, right? You can
use your personal energy to shape the atmosphere of
a room and convey executive presence. First, pause to
notice your personal energy. Then, take stock of the
situation or meeting you're about to enter. Next, decide if your personal energy seems right for that particular situation. What you're looking for is a match.
In some situations, you might want your personal
energy to exude openness and flexibility, in others,
firmness and determination, or compassion and understanding. If your energy and the situation are not
a match, then take a few deep breaths to intentionally
shift your personal energy into alignment with the
current moment.

HAVING THE RIGHT MINDSET. Because Tasha is introspective and continually strives to become more self-aware, she began to notice how her mindset affected her interactions. If her mindset was closed and cautious, she felt guarded and defensive. Conversely, when her mindset was open and receptive, she felt relaxed, interested, and productive. Digging deeper, she realized that no matter the purpose of the meeting or the people involved, she wanted to be authentic and have her mindset match her true self. She began intentionally setting aside preconceived notions about a meeting's content and the people involved. This helped her show up in a true and genuine way, where she could be fully present, and manage her mindset.

Confidently Presenting Yourself

As we've discussed, how you present yourself as a leader makes a big difference. I recall one particular leader who couldn't seem to make up their mind, was easily flustered, and worried incessantly about the tiniest of matters. Neither their words, actions, nor body language conveyed confidence. Ultimately, their lack of self-assuredness led to their downfall. As a leader, you must present yourself with confidence and weave it into everything you do. Let's explore gravitas, communication, and credibility as strategies to confidently present yourself and enhance your executive presence.

GRAVITAS. According to a 2020 *Harvard Business Review* article by Rebecca Newton, having gravitas means you "are taken seriously, your contributions are considered important, and you are trusted and respected." Newton goes on to point out that gravitas "increases your ability to persuade and influence and is likely to fuel the extent to which you rise in an organization." You can think of gravitas as a quality that gives weight to your ideas, presence, and actions. In my experience, behaviors associated with gravitas include confidence, decisiveness, composure, and diplomacy. You've probably experienced a leader with these qualities and noticed how they command the room. Such traits draw people to them, giving weight to their influence and impact.

Displaying grace under fire also demonstrates gravitas. This is the leader who remains calm and composed despite chaos, uncertainty, and stress all around. Their demeanor gives people a sense that everything will be okay. They appear unflappable. Think of a duck gliding across the water. Above the surface, it moves easily and smoothly. Below the surface, there's a lot of action, energy, and movement happening. You can use the duck analogy as a way to self-check your behaviors. What do your above-the-waterline behaviors convey to others—poise and confidence or panic and uncertainty?

Another facet of gravitas is body language. Taking up space, sitting or standing tall, not fidgeting, and holding eye contact are physical manifestations of gravitas. When you're standing, think of elongating your spine, holding your head high, and squaring your shoulders. When sitting, take a relaxed posture that uses up space. Refrain from hunching your shoulders or squeezing yourself into a ball.

Having gravitas doesn't mean showing false bravado or being inauthentic. As I've learned through my years of coaching women, and as Newton points out in her *Harvard Business Review* article, you can develop gravitas while being completely authentic. It begins with the self-awareness work you did in the Activate pillar section of this book and continues as you build your executive presence. Let's look at a quick example to illustrate how gravitas can be authentically cultivated.

Erin, a regional vice president of finance for an automaker, wanted to be more composed, especially when dealing with argumentative people. She works in a tough, high-pressure business where contentious behavior is not unusual. "I remember how, on some days, it got the best of me. Even though I tried to stay calm, it used to be really hard, especially when people were so intent on being challenging and just seemed to want to be difficult."

Erin wanted to remain poised and collected during such encounters because, as she puts it, "I wanted to put my best self forward with people. I knew tough situations came with the territory, but I didn't want to fall prey to argumentative, difficult people. I also didn't want to put on a fake smile. I wanted to feel composed and authentic."

With composure and authenticity as her guiding principles, Erin focused on developing gravitas.

Today, instead of trying to force composure on the outside while seething inside, she uses several strategies discussed in the Activate pillar section of this book. She breathes deeply and notices her thoughts, feelings, and physical sensations. She also purposefully invites her inner champion to be present throughout the day, which helps her maintain genuine composure, even in tough situations.

She also identifies anchor words to think to herself during especially tough meetings. The words act as her internal compass, pointing her toward the behaviors and body language she wants to demonstrate and the impression she wants to make. "I choose a particular anchor word," she explains, "depending on the situation. I've used words such as *calm, receptive, curious, poised,* and *balanced.*" Once she chooses a word, she silently repeats it throughout the interaction or meeting. She also writes the word on a piece of paper to have right in front of her as a visual reminder.

Erin finds that using these strategies helps her maintain composure and convey gravitas. This, in turn, helps her authentically amplify her executive presence, no matter how challenging the situation. "Now, I feel much more in control and at ease. I know that I can stay the course, be calm, and navigate tough situations with authentic inner strength," she says.

Effective Communication. Communicating effectively is much more than words or the exchange of information. It's about *how* you convey your message. I've certainly experienced my fair share of leaders whose communication style was unclear, wishy-washy, vague, verbose, combative, or all of the above. Luckily, I've also experienced leaders whose communication style was clear, compelling, well-organized, and concise.

Communication is central to everyday life—both personally and professionally. You can't opt out of it. Developing strong communication skills is a must—especially for leaders. Think about it. Would you rather be known as vague and verbose or as clear, compelling, and concise? I can recall sitting in board meetings where the leader went on and on, hardly stopping to take a breath. One thought morphed into the next. It was impossible to follow their message and stay focused. How different it is to experience meetings led by those who have developed a clear, well-organized, concise, engaging communication style.

A 2021 *Harvard Business Review* article by Dina Smith discusses the connection between executive presence and communication. "Your presence is inextricably linked to how you communicate. . . . [E]verything you say and do sends a message." The question to ask yourself is, "What is the message I want to send?"

Developing strong communication skills takes practice and patience. To be successful, you have to keep at it until each new skill becomes second nature. If you simply try a new communication skill here or there, you're not going to see meaningful results. It's like going to the gym once a month and hoping for a physical transformation—it's not going to happen. As with the successful acquisition of most skills, consistency and commitment are key.

A former client of mine often brought up the topic of communication in our coaching sessions. She knew she was talkative and was aware that, in any given conversation, she often moved from subject to subject with no direction. She'd lose her train of thought and aimlessly wander from one idea to the next. While she repeatedly expressed a desire to become a better communicator, she dedicated little effort to making it happen. In our coaching sessions, we went over various communication tools, but outside of our sessions, she only sporadically put them to use. While she'd regretfully admit her negligeable attempts to me, she continued to halfheartedly work on the skills we discussed. It was no surprise her communication skills remained largely unimproved and continued to be a point of frustration for her.

If you want to master the foundational skills of executive presence, including effective communication, I encourage you to commit fully to the hard work and time it's going to take. If you're ready to make that commitment, let's consider four strategies for polishing your communication style.

1. The STAR Approach

The STAR approach is a strategy that comes from my human resources days and is often used by job candidates when they're interviewing for a new role. The *S* and *T* stand for *situation* and *task*. The *A* is for *action*, and the *R* is for *results*. I've adopted it with my coaching clients to help them form and deliver short, well-organized messages. Let's say you're leading a project and need to give an update to the executive team. Using the STAR approach, you'd briefly describe the situation or task (the purpose of the project, in this case). That would be followed by a brief summary of recent actions. Then you'd conclude with the results of those actions. The STAR approach gives you a roadmap to follow, allowing your message to be organized, concise, and highly effective. It's also a simple formula that's easy to remember.

2. The Bookend Method

Another strategy I use with my coaching clients is what I call the bookend method. It uses the analogy of a book as a reminder to keep communication crisp and succinct. This is particularly helpful when your audience needs only a high-level summary. First, think about the points you want to convey like chapters in a book. Because your audience only needs a high-level overview, not all chapters are necessary. In fact, an abundance of detail will likely dilute your message and bore your audience. Instead, tell the first and last chapters. The first chapter is the primary message you want your audience to know. The last chapter summarizes next steps. To illustrate, let's go back to the example above in which you need to give a project update to your executive team. The first chapter might sound like, "Project XYZ has been underway since the beginning of this quarter. We've hit all our targets except one, and we're on track with our schedule. The one target we haven't hit is securing an outside technology firm to partner with us." The last chapter might sound like, "We have interviews set up next week with three technology firms and are working closely with our internal IT department to vet them. We're confident we'll have a firm in place by the start of next quarter." That bookend message is clear, concise, and action oriented. It's also free of minutiae and details that aren't necessary for an effective, high-level message.

3. The Power of Pausing

Pausing is another strategy that polishes your communication. Here, you make it a point to pause between sentences and key points. While your pauses may only be a second or two, their effect can be powerful. As discussed in a 2018 *Harvard Business Review* article by Noah Zandan, pauses help you slow down your thinking, which can help keep your thoughts organized. Additionally, pauses help your audience follow your message. As the article points out, a pause can punctuate important points, indicating to the audience that they should listen closely to what you're saying. Even with all its benefits, pausing may feel uncomfortable at first. Still, I encourage you to give it a try. Pick a particular meeting during which to deliberately weave pauses between sentences and key points. It's going to feel awkward at first, but don't give up. The more you practice, the more comfortable it will become.

4. 360 Listening

We certainly don't want to forget the importance of listening. In my experience, leaders who are exceptional listeners have also cultivated their executive presence. They use listening as a way to explore issues and peel back the layers of a situation. Melissa Daimler, in a *Harvard Business Review* article, describes listening as an overlooked leadership tool and suggests three levels of listening: internal, focused, and 360. With internal listening, the focus is on yourself—listening to your own thoughts, worries, responsibilities, etc. Even though you pretend to focus on the other person, you're really not. With focused listening, you shift your attention to the other person but don't fully connect with them. You may be looking at them and nodding your head, but you're missing nuances and important cues. It's only with 360 listening that "the magic happens," as Daimler put it. You're really listening to what the person is saying, how they are saying it, and what they're *not* saying. You hear the pauses they're taking, the level of energy they're putting into their message, the meaning behind their words, etc. With 360 listening, you authentically listen and connect. You can begin to build this skill by picking one person each day with whom you'll practice 360 listening. Afterward, reflect on how it went and how you can continue honing this skill. With dedicated practice, 360 listening will become a natural and powerful part of your communication style.

CREDIBILITY. As a leader, you always want to be credible. Otherwise, your influence and impact will be hampered and people will follow you not because they believe in you or trust you but because they happen to report to you. You're not going to inspire top performance if that's the case. According to *MIT Sloan Management Review*, credibility is characterized by competence and trust. Competence is described as the faith people have in your knowledge, skills, and ability to perform your job. Trust is the belief other people have in your values and dependability. The intersection of credibility and trust is echoed by Ronald Riggio in *Psychology Today:* "Credibility is crucial for leaders because trust is what holds leaders and followers together."

Susan, the director of public relations for a large city, saw firsthand how one particular leader struggled with their knowledge, skills, and overall performance. She recalls how it took a toll on the leader's credibility. She remembers the leader not only having difficulty leading media strategies—a core tenant of this person's job—but also conveying incorrect and contradictory information. Fortunately, Susan didn't have to work for this person for very long—it just *felt* like an eternity. Her experience echoes the research from *MIT Sloan Management Review*: "Leaders lose credibility quickly when they struggle to handle key tasks that are part of their job, have difficulty answering questions about the organization, or make decisions that don't align with the organization and its broader environment." The article goes on to point out that conveying incorrect and contradictory information also quickly erodes credibility.

As you can imagine, Susan's trust in this leader was pretty fragile. Research conducted by Jack Zenger and Joseph Folkman as described in the *Harvard Business Review* states that expertise, judgement, know-how, and experience garner trust. The same article also discusses the importance of consistency in creating trust. This includes keeping promises and commitments as well as being consistent in what you say and how you act. Fostering and nurturing trust is one of the most important responsibilities of a leader. It positions a leader as someone who is respected and admired. It also contributes to their executive presence and overall success.

Fostering trust also has compelling organizational benefits. Research described by ScienceForWork indicates that employees who trust their leaders are less likely to quit, more likely to believe the information their leaders share, and more committed to company decisions. The research also finds that employees are more satisfied with their job and more committed to the organization when they trust their leaders.

There are a number of ways to build trust and foster your credibility. This includes treating others fairly, following company processes and protocols, and involving people in decision-making. From the beginning of her career, Susan noticed that trustworthy leaders make it a habit to communicate the intentions and thought processes behind their actions and decisions. As a result, she started doing this with her teams. She also infused empathy, care, and gratitude into her leadership approach, helping her develop a strong bond with her staff. Another trust-building behavior Susan adopted is giving employees professional growth opportunities. For instance, she now makes it a practice to assign lead roles to less-seasoned team members in order to raise their visibility and stretch their expertise. She also noticed that trustworthy leaders were always open to candid feedback. While it wasn't initially easy, over time, Susan learned to become comfortable with this approach. As a result, she grew into an effective, respected, and credible leader.

Like Tasha, Erin, and Susan, I encourage you to look for ways to weave gravitas, effective communication, and credibility into your daily activities and interactions. Doing so will amplify your executive presence and make you a more effective leader.

Genuinely Connecting

Genuinely connecting with others is an essential part of leadership. After all, it's hard to lead if no one wants to follow you. In my experience, a person can have great technical expertise and plenty of experience, but if they lack the ability to develop relationships and genuinely connect with others, their effectiveness as a leader suffers. As Gallup puts it, "Relationships are fundamental for leaders—they need to encourage others to feel a commitment to the human being who is leading them. Great leaders build genuine connections and trusting relationships with their peers, followers, and networks." That's why genuinely connecting is central to mastering executive presence. Let's consider ways to genuinely connect through approachability, empathy, and appreciation.

> **BE APPROACHABLE.** According to an *Inc.* magazine article, approachability is "an essential professional skill that only gets more important as you ascend the ladder into leadership positions and is expected of managers by their employees." For me, it's akin to setting the table for another person, making it easy for them to talk to and engage with you. And yes, it's true, the greater your title, the more reluctant people may be to engage with you. Being approachable is one way to counterbalance that. A leader can genuinely display approachability in a number of ways, including many of the concepts already discussed in this chapter such as being fully present, bringing the right personal energy, communicating effectively, and listening.
>
> Building solid relationships is a fundamental building block of approachability. One way to do this is to acknowledge and celebrate people's unique, individual contributions and strengths. This creates a

meaningful, genuine connection between you and others, making people feel appreciated and valued.

Sharing your mistakes is another way to become more approachable. Clara, a vice president at a national nonprofit, knows making mistakes is a universal, relatable human experience. Today, she openly shares them, but initially, she was reluctant. She felt vulnerable about opening up and exposing her own missteps, even though intellectually she understood the benefits of sharing them. In the spirit of Collaborative Confidence, she shared her struggle with her trusted friend and colleague Amira. The two supported and championed each other on many occasions and valued their special relationship. Eating lunch together one day, Clara brought up the idea of sharing mistakes as a way to genuinely connect more with her staff.

"Sometimes people put leaders on a pedestal," Amira agreed. "I think sharing mistakes helps employees feel more comfortable."

They brainstormed, and Clara decided she'd test the waters by sharing small, inconsequential mistakes that were easily rectifiable. Over time, and with Amira's encouragement, Clara slowly began sharing more significant mistakes. These efforts began to break down the walls between her and her team members, which is exactly what she had hoped for. Increasingly, she felt more relaxed about sharing her mistakes and the lessons she gained from them. As she learned to be more vulnerable, she sensed her team saw her as more approachable. And she was right—her staff even commented on this new side of her.

You don't have to share your worst mistakes or darkest moments to become more approachable. As Clara's story illustrates, it can be tremendously impactful to share even a few missteps. It gives your team a broader understanding of the challenges and pressures you face. The key is to model what it looks like to learn from your mistakes. It shows that you are imperfect yet resilient. It gives others the courage to share mistakes with you, so everyone on the team can learn, improve, and avoid similar missteps in the future. Sharing mistakes as a team can also help identify processes or checks and balances that can prevent similar mistakes in the future. This ability to share, assess, and improve can have a profound positive impact on you as a leader and on your team's performance. And isn't that what strong leadership is all about?

BE EMPATHETIC. Leadership is more than just hitting the numbers, driving results, and meeting budgets. It's about bringing out the best in people and helping them reach their professional potential. Empathy allows for this type of genuine connection. While some may consider empathy a soft skill, it can fuel real, tangible business outcomes. Let's look at three pieces of supporting research. Catalyst, a global nonprofit committed to advancing women's leadership, surveyed almost 900 employees across several industries and found "empathy is an important driver of employee outcomes such as innovation, engagement, and inclusion—especially in times of crisis. In short, empathy is a must-have in today's workplace." Similarly, a study described in *Inc.* magazine of 5,600 people across 77 organizations says, "The ability of a leader to be empathetic and compassionate had the greatest impact on organizational profitability and productivity." Finally, a 2019 *Harvard Business Review* article by professor Jamil Zaki states that "empathetic workplaces tend to enjoy stronger collaboration, less stress and greater morale, and their employees bounce back more quickly from difficult moments such as layoffs."

Clara appreciates that empathy is the ability to recognize, understand, and feel the emotions and perspectives of other people. She shows empathy in many ways, including listening carefully and offering support when an employee is struggling with an assignment or working under pressure. She communicates empathy not only through her words but also with her body language.

"I make eye contact, nod my head, and usually lean forward a bit," she shares. "I do this because I care and because I want the person to know that I'm paying attention and not distracted."

She also uses 360 listening to understand what the person is *really* saying, including the emotions behind their words.

"I noticed the more I practiced this, the more I was able to pick up on the person's values through the words and phrases they used. I also learned to mirror their language to show I heard and appreciated what they were saying."

Clara is careful not to interrupt unless necessary. Even then, she does so gently.

With a slight laugh she confesses, "It can be hard not to interrupt. It's a muscle I'm continually building. I'm a work in progress."

She gives encouragement and support by offering ideas and resources to help the person through their tough time. Clara is known as an approachable and empathetic leader capable of making genuine connections with people. She is a trusted and therefore effective leader.

EXPRESS APPRECIATION. Given Clara's story so far, it likely comes as no surprise that she's also great at expressing appreciation. There is plenty of research about the workplace benefits of expressing appreciation. As described in a 2021 *Chief Executive* magazine article, an organization with a culture of appreciation makes employees feel five times more valued than a culture that isn't that way. Furthermore, employees are six times more likely to recommend the organization as a great place to work, seven times more likely to stay with the organization throughout their career, and eleven times more likely to feel committed to their job, manager, and company. Additionally, a 2020 *Harvard Business Review* article describes research by Adam Grant and Francesca Gino that shows "when people experience gratitude from their manager, they're more productive."

While this research champions the bottom-line rationale for appreciation, this is not what drives Clara.

"I express gratitude to my team and colleagues because I genuinely appreciate them as individuals," she explains. "The work they do and their commitment to the organization matters to me."

Her appreciation is genuine, sincere, and heartfelt. And because it is real, she is able to genuinely connect with her people on a deep level.

For Clara, expressing appreciation has become an important daily ritual.

"I convey it every chance I get," she says, "in group meetings and during one-on-one interactions. Today, it feels easy and natural, but early in my career, that wasn't the case."

Earlier in her career, Clara's gratitude muscle wasn't very developed, so she took deliberate steps to strengthen it. She recalls that one of her early actions was to look at meeting agendas ahead of time to make a note of what had been accomplished and whom she could thank. Over time, the more she did that, the more it became second nature. Today, she no longer needs to be so deliberate in her preparations because it comes naturally.

She also learned to be specific with her appreciation. Rather than a general, "Thank you for your efforts," she now says, "Thank you for the research and preparation you put into creating XYZ report. It was clearly written and well-organized. It helped lead to an informed decision about the project." Clara learned that it is this specific, personalized appreciation that makes people feel truly valued.

While Clara is great at expressing verbal appreciation, she also recognizes the power of thank-you notes. She regularly sends emails of appreciation to her team, peers, and colleagues. On special occasions, she sends handwritten notes. She recalls one particular example in which a high-profile project was about to go off the rails due to unforeseen circumstances but an employee stepped up to work extra hours and weekends to get it completed. She sent the employee a handwritten note expressing her sincere appreciation. She also sends handwritten notes at the end of each fiscal year thanking her direct reports for all their contributions and efforts.

"I also make it a point to let my CEO know my team's contributions, efforts, and hard work," she says. "I want the CEO to know how much I appreciate my team. I also include the bottom-line impact of my team's efforts because I know tangible business results are important."

Clara continually weaves approachability, empathy, and appreciation into her everyday work. As a result, she genuinely connects with others. This, in turn, allows her to authentically amplify her executive presence. She effectively models the best behaviors she expects from

herself and others. Over time, this can have a powerful, positive impact on a workplace's culture. It can create the kind of atmosphere
where people thrive. Like Clara, you too can amplify your executive
presence by genuinely connecting with people. Be approachable, show
genuine empathy, and express authentic appreciation. Deliberately
look for ways to weave these practices into your daily interactions.

Developing executive presence is a key driver of your professional
success and career trajectory. If you dismiss it as an unnecessary
soft skill, you run the risk of your career stalling out. Remember,
78 percent of CEOs, C-suite leaders, and executives believe a lack
of executive presence can hamper a person's career. Don't take that
chance. Instead, commit to strengthening your executive presence.
Remember the stories and experiences of Tasha, Erin, Susan, and
Clara. Learn from them and apply the strategies described in this
chapter to authentically show up, confidently present yourself, and
genuinely connect with others.

First Impressions

First impressions play an important role in executive presence—and we all know how much those can matter. A study
written on PsyPost states that "a single glance of a person's
face for just 33 to 100 ms [is] sufficient to form a first impression." Whoa! If the speed of that takes your breath away,
another study described in *Inc.* reveals you have a leisurely
27 seconds to make a first impression. The study goes on to
reveal that 69 percent of people form a first impression even
before a person speaks. As described by the Association for
Psychological Science, impressions can influence how you
view someone's trustworthiness, competence, goals, values,

and beliefs. First impressions also tend to stick, making it challenging to change them. Even if the impression isn't accurate, its likely to endure. This all means that first impressions have the power to easily shape how you're perceived, including your executive presence.

Impressions are formed by many factors, including how a person looks and sounds, their body language and facial expressions, their attitude, and how they dress. When you meet someone, especially for the first time, be mindful of the impression you want to make. Use your body language, including eye contact, smiling, and shaking hands firmly. Be aware of your posture, too. In certain situations, such as in an interview or in a negotiation, you might want to sit up straight and take up a lot of space. In other situations, such as an informal work gathering, you might sit in a more relaxed manner. Dress the part by choosing attire that fits the occasion and projects the impression you want to convey. Use language that engages the other person. This may include showing interest in them by asking questions, complimenting them, or mirroring their words. Listening is another way to engage and show you're paying attention. Remember the executive presence strategies you learned in this chapter—authentically show up, confidently present yourself, and genuinely connect—to influence other people's first impressions of you.

Chapter 6

Seize Opportunities to Showcase Your Leadership

The trajectory of Nancy's career was fueled by a strong work ethic, tremendous expertise, clear executive presence, and making her accomplishments known. It was this last item, though, that didn't come naturally. In the early years of her career, she often struggled to make her contributions visible to others. It was frustrating and held her back. Over time, however, she learned to artfully showcase her accomplishments. Mastering this skill contributed to her meteoric rise from line cook to chief operating officer at a regional hospital—but not without "some bumps and bruises along the way," as Nancy recalls with a slight chuckle and broad smile.

Despite a growing list of achievements in her various positions, Nancy vividly recalls the day Barbara, a trusted colleague, told her how others perceived her. It was toward the end of a day, while they were sitting in a conference room overlooking the hospital's rose garden. Nancy was complaining about a recent accomplishment of hers being overlooked. They had just come from a leadership team meeting where the senior vice president of the information technology department hadn't recognized her efforts on a recent project. After hearing her out, Barbara gently said, "Nancy, unfortunately, many people don't know all the great things you're doing for the hospital. It's like you're invisible to the leadership team." While people had a favorable impression of Nancy as a person, Barbara went on to explain, they didn't have a clear understanding of Nancy's impact as a leader. They didn't connect business results back to her.

This was startling news that devastated and angered Nancy, making her head spin. At first, she couldn't make sense of it. *How can this be? This is so unfair,* she thought.

"I'm such a hard worker and always give it my all," she told Barbara, who wholeheartedly agreed. Barbara expressed genuine empathy and support, reminding Nancy of other tough situations they'd helped each other through. Even though the news hit hard, she appreciated Barbara's honesty and knew Barbara was in her corner. They decided to collaborate on what Nancy could do to change the situation. As they continued having open, honest, and vulnerable conversations, something became clear: Nancy needed to become better at strategically showcasing her leadership skills and accomplishments. She had to connect the dots for people to clearly see the results she was generating, important decisions she was making, risks she was taking, and teams she was building. She was great at what she did, and it was time for others to see it. But shining a spotlight on her accomplishments made her uncomfortable. Still, something had to change. With no small degree of trepidation, Nancy began to stretch her comfort zone and amplify her talents and contributions. Fortunately, by her side and encouraging her all the way was her trusted friend and colleague Barbara. Together, they engaged in what is at the heart of Collaborative Confidence: women championing each other. With attentive care and Barbara's help, Nancy overcame this challenge and became recognized as a strong leader.

Self-Promotion Challenges Women Face

In the previous chapter, you read about executive presence and learned specific strategies for cultivating it. Like Nancy came to understand, if you don't take measures to visibly demonstrate your executive presence, it holds limited power. But showcasing one's leadership is not necessarily easy for women. For some, it feels like self-promotion—and the record is pretty clear that women tend to be uncomfortable with that. I've had my own share of struggles showcasing my accomplishments. I recall after getting my doctorate degree how I waited a full year to add *Dr.* Heather Backstrom to my website—a full year! Even though I had earned the degree, with a 4.0 magna cum laude GPA no less, I was still reluctant to put it out there for others to see. In comparison, a male friend at school put doctor on his website immediately. He didn't struggle with letting the world know of his great and well-earned accomplishment. How come I did?

My example is consistent with research on the differences between men and women when it comes to self-promotion. Christine Exley and Judd Kessler researched this phenomenon by running various versions of the same test to measure workers' performance, confidence, and self-promotion. They describe their findings in a 2019 *Harvard Business Review* article: "We found that men engage in substantially more self-promotion than women." Exley and Kessler were particularly interested in the self-promotion gender gap because of its pervasiveness and impact on professionals' jobs and career trajectories. They theorize that "those of us who do more self-promotion may have better chances of being hired, being promoted, and getting a raise or bonus."

Yet, for women, self-promotion can be a double bind. Spotlighting accomplishments and experiences is crucial, but if a woman overdoes it, she risks being seen in an unfavorable light. As Florida International University (FIU) shares in a blog post:

> On the path to getting ahead in organizations, men and women leaders need to behave in ways that are ambitious, self-confident, independent, [and] competent . . . in order to be promoted and be seen as "leaders." However, robust research suggests that, when these behaviors are enacted by women (but not by men), [it] can lead to a social and economic backlash. Indeed, dozens of studies over decades have shown that this puts women in a precarious position—if women are dominant or assertive, they often become labeled as "too bossy," whereas men who engage in the exact same behaviors would not be punished, and in fact may be rewarded and promoted for their "leadership."

What a tightrope women have to walk! As an article in the *Atlantic* puts it, "Women must learn to master the art of appearing both sure of themselves and modest. Too much of the latter, and women's achievements get overlooked. Too much of the former, and they can face what experts refer to as the 'backlash effect'—social and professional sanctions for failing to conform to gender norms."

Not surprising, the double-bind phenomenon occurs in politics, too. Yoshikuni Ono, a political scientist at Waseda University in Tokyo, is quoted in a 2021 BBC article saying, "Female candidates face a more difficult time figuring out what would be the good strategy to win the election or get more support from people, because deviating from gender stereotypes might be bad for women. At the same time, conforming to gender stereotypes punishes them as well. So, it seems very difficult for female politicians to find the sweet spot when they plan their strategy." The BBC article adds that the double bind is all the more treacherous for women of color: "Black women are stereotyped as too abrasive, and Asian women are stereotyped as too docile to lead."

Researchers Wei Zheng, Ronit Kark, and Alyson Meister, writing in the *Harvard Business Review,* explore the double bind between being warm and nice compared with competent and tough. They identify four paradoxes women leaders routinely face: they must be demanding yet caring, be authoritative yet participative, advocate for themselves yet serve others, and maintain distance yet be approachable.

Nancy came to understand that she was too caring, participative, service-oriented, and approachable—and her stature as a leader was suffering because of it. While I'm sure we can agree these are important and valuable traits, when tipped too far in one direction, they cause an imbalance. This imbalanced approach meant Nancy's achievements and impact were being largely overlooked.

As she continued to stretch her comfort zone, her inner critics became quite chatty, causing her to slip back into old habits. She shared this with Barbara.

"Just the thought of being more direct and authoritative makes my heart race and body tense up. I feel so anxious, insecure, and uncertain." As a way to regain her footing and increase her self-awareness, Barbara suggested she tune in to the interplay among her thoughts, feelings, and physical sensations. So, when Nancy noticed a negative thought, she immediately checked how she was feeling. Then she changed the thought to something more positive and watched how it affected her feelings. She also paid attention to physical sensations and used them as an internal barometer. There wasn't a specific sequence to this—sometimes it was a physical sensation she noticed first, then the feeling, and then the thought—but regardless, she was starting to see patterns. She complemented this with other strategies. She often used deep breathing and the physical sensation of rubbing her thumb and a finger together, along with connecting to her inner champion. She also relied on her core values of resourcefulness, determination, and optimism to propel her forward. The more she practiced, the less potent her inner critics became.

Although embarrassed to admit it, Nancy confided in Barbara that despite all her hard work to silence her inner critics, they often got the best of her. Barbara empathized and shared her own experiences with "those annoying inner critics." Just knowing that Barbara faced a similar battle made Nancy feel better. Over time, Nancy learned to push through and stay committed to her goals.

There are many inspiring stories of female leaders learning to successfully navigate the tightrope of self-promotion. Angie Hicks, cofounder of Angi (formerly Angie's List), started her business by going door-to-door promoting herself and her company's services. As she has publicly stated, this was her worst nightmare. Scott Brenton, COO of Angie's List from 1999 to 2012, is quoted in *Indianapolis Monthly*, saying, "Stepping into the spotlight was absolutely challenging for her, but she understands that's where her mark on the business could most be felt. She didn't set out to make a name for herself as a public figure—perhaps because of that people think she's genuine." It's clear she had to stretch her comfort zone in order to be successful and grow her business.

Both Nancy and Angie had to leave their comfort zones to find success. Before we examine what it means to be visible, let's consider the mindset changes this requires. After all, you can have the most perfect set of strategies laid out, but if your mindset is stuck, then so are you.

Reframe Your Mindset

Because women tend to shy away from activities that showcase their skills and achievements, the first step is a mindset shift. If the idea of self-promotion makes your skin crawl, then let's reframe it. I like to think of self-promotion as clear communication. As you read in chapter 5, communication is a fundamental ingredient of executive presence. It's also a lens from which you can reframe self-promotion. When you simply and clearly convey your accomplishments, skills, and impact, you're being a clear communicator.

Another reframe is to recognize that you're a role model for other women. When you see yourself as a role model, it helps you feel more comfortable about spotlighting your accomplishments. If you have difficulty doing it for yourself, think about all the other women you'll inspire. Each time you own your accomplishments, you pave the way for other women to feel comfortable doing the same. Research by the Self-Promotion Gap, a consortium of women-owned companies, found "a majority of women (83 percent) have been inspired by hearing women talk about their successes and accomplishments, but seven in ten women (69 percent) would rather minimize their successes than tell people about them." Aspire to be a source of inspiration for other women. In the spirit of Collaborative Confidence, let's move the needle so many more than only three out of ten women are comfortable sharing their success.

Visibility

Visibility is vitally important to a woman's career advancement. When researchers Shelley J. Correll and Lori Nishiura Mackenzie asked 240 senior leaders of a Silicon Valley technology company to name the most critical success factors that got them promoted to their level, there was one that overshadowed all the others: visibility. As described in their *Harvard Business Review* article, "More than technical competence, business results or team leadership, these leaders agreed visibility is the most important factor for advancement. . . . In our observation, visibility is a complex interaction of perceived skills (particularly technical and leadership ones), access to stretch assignments, and being known (and liked) by influential senior leaders within informal networks. All three are necessary for advancement."

Let's consider the following strategies for raising your visibility: accentuate your physical presence, artfully claim credit, speak up, and manage interruptions.

ACCENTUATE PHYSICAL PRESENCE

I was once at a professional networking event where I witnessed a very talented, high-profile female attorney physically shrink herself in front of the entire room. As she stood up to make an announcement, she pushed her backside against the wall, crossed one leg over the other, and held an arm across her body, linking it with the other arm, like a shield. As successful as she was, she diminished her presence and visibility. She had no command of the room. I like to refer to this kind of behavior as a microdiminishment—the seemingly small ways women diminish themselves. Over time, these behaviors rack up and erode a woman's visibility, no matter how talented she is.

Conversely, have you ever been in the presence of a woman leader who exudes a commanding presence?

I have. It's impressive and inspiring. Women who command a room know how to use their physical presence to stand out. They sit up straight and choose a prominent place in the room to be. They take up space while seated and hold their heads upright and steady. They don't fidget. They smile comfortably and make eye contact. Adopt these types of physical behaviors and watch how it raises your visibility so that you too command the room with confidence and ease.

Strategically choosing where you sit in meetings also accentuates your physical presence. Rather than grabbing a chair around the perimeter of the room, choose to sit at the conference room table. If you're used to being on the perimeter, this may feel uncomfortable at first and your inner critics may try to persuade you otherwise. Still, stretch your comfort zone by remaining committed until it feels natural. Where you sit when you're leading a meeting matters, too. Be aware that sitting at the head of a table or somewhere alongside it can send different messages. For instance, sitting at the head of the table may telegraph being in command and in charge, while sitting alongside it may convey a participative and collaborative atmosphere. Be aware of the message you want to send and pick where to sit based on it.

Video conferences have never been more common and will only continue to be a workplace mainstay. When you're in a video conference, do your best to have your camera set in a way that people can see you well. Be sure to position the camera so your face is comfortably framed.

ARTFULLY CLAIM CREDIT

On many occasions, I've witnessed women give public credit to their teams without mentioning themselves. I had a client who was always quick to point out the contributions and achievements of her team because she genuinely appreciated them and didn't want their efforts to be overlooked. Trouble was, her own impact was being overlooked. When given a compliment, she'd often reply along the lines of, "Well, the credit goes to my team. They put in a lot of hours and worked hard." Through our coaching, she learned this kind of response is a microdiminishment that minimizes her impact and visibility. Today, when complimented, her replies are along the lines of, "Thank you. I enjoyed leading XYZ effort and am proud of my team." This way, she takes a balanced approach that positions herself as a successful leader *and* acknowledges her team.

Here are some other balanced approach examples: Rather than saying, "It was a team effort," say, "It was great leading the team to a successful outcome." Or rather than, "It was no big deal, I have a great team," say, "My team is great, and I was happy to lead them through it." Artfully claiming credit in this way is a balanced and factual representation of your efforts as well as your team's. The next time you're acknowledged for doing good work, be careful to give a balanced response so you claim credit for yourself while acknowledging your team's efforts.

All too many times, I've seen women give away their credit through their very own words about themselves, which is another kind of microdiminishment. Once, at a conference, a businesswoman seated near me made light of a prestigious award she had won. As the meeting started, introductions were made, and a male professional said he had been named as a top one hundred leader by a prominent industry magazine. A few introductions later, the businesswoman said she had also been named in the same list. Then, under her breath, she added, "I don't know why." What?! Although it wasn't much more than a whisper, those seated near her heard it, including me. I was shocked. She should have owned her accomplishment. Still, I empathized because this is something I have had to work on myself. Over time, I have learned to self-edit so that I don't dilute my accomplishments. Next time you reference an accomplishment, such as an award or professional accolade, simply state it and stop talking. If you're drawn to add anything further, let it be along the lines of, "I feel very honored" or "It was a thrill to be recognized."

Another way to claim credit is to respond to a compliment with two words: thank you. I've seen women minimize themselves by following a compliment by saying, "Oh, I could have done it better" or "I thought I bored people during my presentation" or

"Anyone could have done it." If receiving a compliment is difficult for you, challenge yourself to simply say thank you the next time it happens.

If only saying thank you seems insufficient, then add on, "That means a lot to me" or "I appreciate you saying that." At first, this kind of self-editing may not feel comfortable or natural. You can learn to become comfortable with it by engaging in Collaborative Confidence, where you and another woman practice giving each other real, genuine compliments. In return say, "Thank you." The more you practice, the more apt you'll be at gracefully and comfortably receiving a compliment.

SPEAK UP

I once coached a senior director of accounting services for a government agency. She never spoke up in meetings and almost always sat in the back of the room or in a chair against the wall. It was hurting her career and she knew it. When her 360-degree assessment came back, the volume of comments about her invisibility was no surprise. While people said they had faith in her technical skills, they questioned her leadership effectiveness. The comments were along the lines of the following:

> I think her point of view is important and it would be good to hear it, but she hardly ever shares it.

> It's hard to know what she's thinking because the only time she speaks up is when she's asked, otherwise she just sits there.

> She's so quiet in meetings, which is surprising given her leadership role.

We discussed this feedback in our coaching sessions. While she said she understood their point of view, she initially resisted doing anything about it. "I don't want to talk just for the sake of talking. Plus, a lot of times, I don't have an opinion and don't just want to make one up."

While her point was valid, there are numerous useful ways to speak up and contribute to a conversation. Over time, as we explored various options, she warmed up to the idea that she could add value beyond stating an opinion. One strategy we discussed was asking clarifying questions. She came to appreciate that clarifying questions benefit everyone because they lead to better understanding—and it's a great way to raise her visibility. Another tactic we discussed was to connect the dots between what two people have said by saying something such as, "Chris, what you said sounds similar to Tracy's point of view." She agreed this would raise her visibility while helping the group see similar points of view. We also talked about comparing or contrasting people's ideas as a way to benefit the group while raising her visibility. This might sound like, "Chris, what you said seems different than what Tracy shared. Am I hearing both of you correctly?" These types of questions also create the opportunity for continued group dialogue. Finally, we also explored how she could bring someone into the conversation who hadn't spoken yet. For instance, if the topic at hand related to someone's area of work, she might say, "Chris, it strikes me that this affects your team's workload. What are your thoughts?" She saw how this would raise her visibility while enriching the group's discussion. As we explored these strategies and their benefits to both her and the team, her resistance faded. She made a commitment to incorporate at least one strategy into each meeting she attended. Over time, she saw how it benefitted the quality and depth of group discussions. She also enjoyed a great boost when comments on a subsequent 360-degree report complimented her for the changes she had made.

SKILLFULLY MANAGE INTERRUPTIONS

All of us have been interrupted and have been guilty of interrupting others. Still, research shows that men interrupt women much more than women interrupt men.

So, what is a woman to do? How can she skillfully handle interruptions? Here are a few ideas:

- Politely let the interrupter know you're not done by saying, "Let me finish my thought" or "One moment, I'm not quite done." During the October 2020 televised vice-presidential debate, then candidate Kamala Harris said to then Vice President Mike Pence when he interrupted her, "Mr. Vice President, I'm speaking" and "If you don't mind letting me finish, then we can have a conversation." According to a CBS News tally, Pence interrupted Harris ten times, while she interrupted him only five.

- Use body language to signal you're not done talking. Sit up straighter or gesture with one of your hands, for example.

- Toss the interrupter a bit of a compliment by saying, "Oh, I see you're just as enthusiastic about this as I am. As I was saying. . ."

- Concur with the interrupter by saying, "I hear you have concerns, as do I. Let me add. . ."

- Continue speaking. When I've done this, the interrupter does stop talking, but I'm fully aware that it may make me look bossy and aggressive. So, it's a tactic I use sparingly and only after other efforts have failed.

You can also preempt interruptions through preparation. For instance, you can decide ahead of a meeting that you'll remain calm and composed even if you're interrupted. That way, you'll remain clearheaded and be in a better position to navigate interruptions. Another preemptive strategy is to set up some rules of engagement. Before a meeting, suggest that after an idea is put on the table, the group go around the room listening to each person one by one without interruption. You can use a similar strategy during a meeting. When you notice a chorus of interruptions, you can pause the conversation and suggest people speak one at a time. You can even have fun with it by suggesting interrupters cough up a dollar for each infraction. Or you can designate the use of a talking stick, where a person is only allowed to speak if they're the holder of the stick. In place of an actual stick, you can use any available object such as a pen, stapler, or desk accessory.

Use all of these strategies to raise your visibility and showcase your accomplishments. Accentuating your physical presence, artfully claiming credit, speaking up, and managing interruptions will raise your stature as a capable, talented leader. As you master these skills, consider partnering with other women in the spirit of Collaborative Confidence. Like Nancy, pair up with another woman so you're not doing it all on your own. You can bounce ideas around, come up with more strategies, celebrate wins, and commiserate when things don't turn out quite as you planned. Encourage each other as you incorporate visibility strategies into your everyday work.

Because organizational cultures and societal expectations change slowly, we also have to point out the responsibility companies have to spotlight women leaders. Like women themselves, organizations must commit to raising the visibility of their women leaders. We'll explore this more in chapter 8, but stretch assignments and sponsorship are two ways companies can help women leaders.

Fatima was the senior director of finance at a large nonprofit. She was accomplished and well respected. Executive leadership recognized her talents, along with her team-player spirit. As a result, her boss began giving her stretch assignments. The first one was giving a portion of the monthly board presentation. While Fatima was responsible for preparing the board packet, presenting was another matter. The next stretch assignment was serving on a cross-functional committee for a new telecommunications system. This gave Fatima deep insight into the infrastructure of the organization, as well as how complex decisions got made. Then, she was given the assignment to streamline the budget process to make it more efficient. This required her gathering input from internal customers, coalescing their feedback, and making recommendations to her boss. All these assignments challenged and stretched her skills and raised her visibility. Ultimately, they contributed to her promotion to vice president of finance. Organizations can strategically use stretch assignments to get critical work done, build employees' skills, and raise their visibility. It takes a concerted, deliberate commitment on the part of organizations to look beyond an employee's current expertise and mine for what can be developed. If you haven't had a stretch assignment, or if your company isn't in the habit of offering them, take charge by asking for one yourself.

While a stretch assignment helped Fatima's career, having a sponsor is another way to afford women leaders visibility. Sponsors are typically senior leaders who advocate on behalf of a rising star. Sponsors can tout a woman's accomplishments, play up her potential, connect her to people in their network, and recommend her for bigger roles. However, according to professor Herminia Ibarra in a 2019 *Harvard Business Review* article, "Too few women are reaching the top of their organizations, and a big reason is that they are not getting the high-stakes assignments that are prerequisite for a shot at the C-suite. Often, this is due to a lack of powerful sponsors demanding and ensuring that they get these stepping-stone jobs." This is a call to action for organizations to leverage sponsorships as a way to propel more capable, talented women into executive roles while accomplishing important company work.

Now is the time to seize opportunities to artfully showcase your leadership. While it may not feel comfortable and you may face bumps along the way, like Nancy did, the payoff can be tremendous. It can propel your career forward. You will also be an important role model for other women. If you're still feeling trepidatious, let your ability to inspire other women motivate you. Also, remember that engaging in Collaborative Confidence is a great way to partner with other women for support. You've worked hard to get here. You've already activated your self-awareness and amplified your executive presence. Now is the time to artfully showcase your leadership.

Justice Sotomayor Takes On Interruptions at the Supreme Court

Remarkably, even on the Supreme Court, women justices are interrupted more often than male justices. Speaking at New York University School of Law in October 2021, Supreme Court Justice Sonia Sotomayor recalled a 2017 study by Tonja Jacobi and Dylan Schweers of Northwestern University that found female justices are interrupted more often than their male counterparts regardless of seniority or other factors. A *Harvard Business Review* article by the study's authors provides additional details:

> Male justices interrupt the female justices approximately three times as often as they interrupt each other during oral arguments....

[A]s more women join the court, the reaction of the male justices has been to increase the interruptions of the female justices. Male justices are now interrupting female justices at double-digit rates per term, but the reverse is almost never true. In the last 12 years, during which women made up, on average, 24 percent of the bench, 32 percent of interruptions were of female justices but only 4 percent were by female justices.

How did the female justices navigate what I can only imagine must have been an exasperating experience? It seems that the passage of time and observation have helped. Jacobi and Schweers's article explains that the longer female justices sit on the court, the more adept they become at handling interruptions. The researchers observe, "Time on the court gives women a chance to learn how to avoid being interrupted, by talking more like men." The authors describe how less-tenured female justices politely say phrases such as "May I ask," "Can I ask," or "Excuse me." As their time on the bench progresses, they gradually let such politeness go by the wayside and adapt speech patterns similar to the male justices.

Fortunately, this research did not go unnoticed. In fact, it distinctly changed the dynamic of the court. In speaking at NYU Law School, Sotomayor adds, "After reports of that finding came out, our chief judge was much more sensitive to ensuring that people were, if not interrupted, at least that he was playing referee when interruptions happened and ensuring that people got back to the judge who was interrupted." The research also had a ripple effect on the behaviors of the individual justices as well, Sotomayor explains: "I also found that my colleagues are much more sensitive than they were before. You see us even now, when we're speaking, a judge will say, 'I'm sorry did I interrupt you?' and if you say, 'I was going to finish something,' they say, 'Please go ahead.' That did not happen as much before." She went on to acknowledge that interruptions are commonplace in society: "Regrettably, that's a dynamic that exists not just on the Court but in our society in general. Most of the time, women say things and they're not heard in the same way as men who might say the identical thing."

While the Supreme Court had the benefit of a study, a chief justice who became more aware of the court's dynamics, and other justices who demonstrated self-awareness, I venture to say that the rest of us are not so lucky. Organizational psychologist and author Adam Grant details workplace interruptions in a 2021 *Washington Post* article describing a study of US senators by Victoria L. Brescoll. As Grant explains, the study found senators with status and influence talked more on the Senate floor, but only if they were men. That's because the female senators didn't want to come across as too dominant and controlling. Grant adds, "Gender stereotypes persist. People expect men to be assertive and ambitious but women to be caring and other-oriented. A man who runs his mouth and holds court is a confident expert. A woman who talks is aggressive or pushy."

He went further by describing political science research by Christopher F. Karpowitz and Tali Mendelberg from their book, *The Silent Sex: Gender, Deliberation, and Institutions,* which observes how the gender makeup of a group affects the amount of time a woman talks. Summarizing this research, Grant says, "When groups of five make democratic decisions, if only one member is a woman, she speaks 40 percent less than each of the men. Even if the group has a majority of three women, they each speak 36 percent less than each of the two men. Only in groups with four women do they each finally take up as much airtime as the one man. In too many teams and too many workplaces, women face the harsh reality that it is better to stay silent and be thought polite than speak up and jeopardize their careers."

Chapter 7

Spotlight Contributions and Ideas of Other Women

During former president Obama's first term, the vast majority of his top aides and cabinet members were men. They easily exerted their influence in meetings, while top female aides found it hard to achieve the same stature, despite their stellar credentials and extensive political experience. Not only did these women struggle to get their voices heard in meetings, but they struggled to be included in them in the first place. That meant they were left out of policy decisions, strategic calculations, and other matters of national and global significance. As described by Juliet Eilperin in her September 2016 *Washington Post* article about the situation, "Women complained of having to elbow their way into important meetings. And when they got in their voices were sometimes ignored."

These strong, intelligent women were not about to be deterred, though. They came together and adopted an imaginative strategy they called "amplification." When a female aide made a point in a meeting, another woman repeated it, giving credit back to her. As reported by Eilperin, an anonymous Obama aide said, "We just started doing it and made a purpose of doing it. It was an everyday thing." As the women continued amplifying each other, over time, Obama noticed and began calling on them. The women's brilliant strategy raised their voices, visibility, and impact. They were no longer on the sidelines; they were at the center of everything.

Fortunately, by Obama's second term, his administration had changed significantly, with gender parity among his top aides rising. As Valerie Jarrett, who served in both of Obama's administrations, told the *Washington Post*, "It's fair to say that there was a lot of testosterone flowing in those early days. Now, we have a little more estrogen that provides a counterbalance." Additionally, the tenor of the second administration was influenced because a number of the aides from Obama's first term moved on to other work. Looking more broadly at Obama's second administration, about half of all the White House departments (ranging from the National Security Council to the Office of Legislative Affairs) were led by women. This example illustrates that while amplification is a simple concept, it can have a tremendous, lasting impact and bring women out of the shadows and into the spotlight where they belong. Interestingly, Eilperin's *Washington Post* article had an unexpected ripple effect, which she wrote about in a follow-up article a month later. In her second article, Eilperin describes how women across the country, from various professional industries, contacted her saying they too had adopted amplification.

I've personally shared the White House amplification story in workshops and women's circles I lead. Participants are immediately captivated. It's so relatable because women's voices, opinions, and presence are often overlooked and overshadowed. As a tool, amplification is also easy to adopt, effective, and collaborative. Women appreciate the reciprocal nature of it. No longer do they have to shoulder the hard work of getting noticed alone. They now have allies to champion them. Several weeks after a workshop I facilitated, a participant contacted me, excited to share that she had introduced amplification to a handful of her female colleagues at work.

"I was so inspired by the Obama story, I could hardly wait to tell my female colleagues. I can't tell you how many times we're in meetings and can hardly get our ideas across because the men interrupt all the time and we get overshadowed. Even though we're partners and theoretically equal, it just doesn't seem equal when we get sidelined."

She was a lawyer at a large law firm where the majority of the attorneys were men. Once the other female attorneys learned about amplification, they were enthusiastic about practicing it. Their male counterparts took notice. The workshop participant also shared an unexpected bonus the women in her firm experienced: they felt more confident and empowered.

"The effect has been so powerful," she told me. "We all feel more equal in meetings, and we're included more in decisions. We don't have to scramble to get heard, and our opinions are taken more seriously. I know I feel a lot more confident, and so do the other women." She went on to say their efforts had a ripple effect, too. As even more women in other parts of the firm got wind of amplification, they started doing it, too. She marveled at how something so simple could generate such a wide-ranging impact.

The Impact of Amplification

The impact of amplification has been studied by researchers Kristin Bain, Tamar A. Kreps, Nathan L. Meikle, and Elizabeth R. Tenney. In a 2021 *Harvard Business Review* article, they discuss three questions: Does amplifying someone make that person's ideas seem better? Does amplifying someone else make the amplifier look good? Can amplification be used in groups to help underrepresented voices be heard? The bottom-line answer to each of these questions is yes. Using the term *voicer* to refer to the person who makes an initial comment or suggestion, the researchers report, "The voicer's idea was [perceived as] better when [a] team member amplified it, and. . . that the voicer was more influential and high-status in the group." The research also reveals that the person doing the amplification gains status as well. "When you lift up a teammate by amplifying their idea, you can uplift yourself, too," the research indicates.

The researchers were also curious about what happens if men amplify men as well as women. Across the board, they say "amplification was beneficial for everyone." Amplification appears to elevate the ideas, opinions, and presence of anyone who is being overlooked. "Voicers who were amplified looked high-status compared to voicers who weren't amplified, whether they were men or women. And teammates who amplified others looked high-status, too, compared to those who responded in any other way, whether they were men or women." Amplification appears to offer a win-win solution all around. The researchers theorize, "[Our] findings suggest that women (and potentially members of other groups underrepresented in organizations, particularly at the highest levels) can use amplification to improve equity and inclusion. When a woman amplifies a woman, two women benefit: both the one whose contribution now has a vocal supporter, and the one who looks magnanimous and generous for recognizing a colleague."

Now is the time to put amplification into practice at your workplace. You can start informally by choosing to amplify at least one other woman in your organization. Take a look at your upcoming meetings and keep your ears attuned for opportunities to authentically amplify other women. Endorse or acknowledge other women's ideas and redirect conversations that go astray. Don't let the credit a female colleague deserves evaporate or be attributed to another person. You might say, "Natalie's idea about XYZ is intriguing. Let's hear more from her" or "Bob, that idea sounds exactly like what Natalie said a moment ago." As you read in chapter 6—and as you've likely experienced yourself—women tend to be interrupted more often than their male counterparts. Redirect the conversation when female coworkers are interrupted. You might say, "I'd like Natalie to finish her thought," "I'd like to go back to Natalie because she was interrupted," or "I think Natalie was in the middle of saying something that she didn't get to finish. I'd like to hear her out." You can play with both subtle and more overt ways of giving credit and redirecting conversations. Take into account the situation and the people involved to make the best judgement about how to handle things.

You can also put amplification into action by teaming up with another woman or a select group of women. Look around your office and decide with whom you'd like to collaborate. Share the Obama administration story as an inspirational starting point. Together, decide the avenue you want to use to amplify each other. Each work situation is unique, just like each individual, so utilize amplification in a way that best suits the situation and the people involved. For example, there might be a particular monthly meeting where women are regularly sidelined. Start there. Or maybe there's a notorious interrupter in your office and you take it upon yourself to redirect the conversation when you're around that person. Or perhaps you're fortunate enough to have an established group of trusted female colleagues who are ready to dive into amplification full force. Regardless of how you choose to go about it, the power of amplification is fueled by action. Don't let another day go by. Take the reins and make the change you want to see a reality.

Amplification Characteristics

Amplification is at its best when certain characteristics are present. One is that you're in it for the long haul. You can't amplify another woman for a meeting or two and then quit. Success comes through long-term commitment and repetition. That's what makes it potent and gives it sticking power. Had the women in Obama's administration only amplified each other a few times, I wonder if he would have noticed and if changes would have come from it. Seems doubtful to me.

Seeing amplification as an investment is also an important characteristic. Amplification is an investment in you, other women, and your organization's culture. Similar to a financial investment, it has an ROI. Like the female Obama aides and the women at the law firm, their presence and impact were elevated because of amplification. The overall tenor of both organizations changed for the better, too. Like any investment, the more you put in, the more you get out. Every day, look for opportunities to invest further in amplification. Ask a woman her opinion in a meeting, encourage a woman to sit in a prominent place in the room, publicly acknowledge another woman for her efforts, redirect the conversation back to a woman when the focus has been stolen from her, or recommend a woman for a meaningful assignment. Investing every day in amplification increases the ROI for you, other women, and your workplace culture.

Another important characteristic of amplification is authenticity. It's always best to genuinely and authentically amplify another woman. It's not about repeating what she said for the sake of it. It's not about asking her opinion just to ask. It's not about including her in a meeting just to include her. People see through disingenuous acts. This can erode the ripple effect of amplification. Authenticity gives amplification power and strength, helping the women you amplify be seen as valuable contributors whose opinions and presence hold weight.

Finally, amplification relies on mutual trust. You trust another woman to amplify you, and she trusts you to do the same for her. Even when you're not together, amplification means you'll still give her credit for her ideas, endorse her expertise, or recommend her for a plumb assignment. Mutual trust is the glue that binds your commitment to each other no matter the circumstances.

Amplification Strategies

So far, we've emphasized giving credit to women and redirecting conversations back to women as amplification strategies. These are indeed powerful and impactful. Let's add some other strategies, too.

> **PLUS-ONE EVENTS.** The next time you're invited to a professional event (whether an association meeting, gala, philanthropic benefit, or other event) bring along a female colleague as your plus-one guest. I know a woman leader who does this every time she's invited to an event in which attendees can bring a guest. Rather than bringing her spouse, she brings a female colleague. "I want the women in my organization to get every chance to network and make a name for themselves," she tells me. "It's especially important because we work in a male-dominated field." This strategy not only elevates a female colleague's visibility, but it telegraphs to others the woman's value and importance to the organization. As an additional

benefit, women get exposed to more people, information, and situations, which contributes to professional growth.

IMPORTANT MEETINGS. You can bring a female colleague to an important business meeting. For instance, if you're presenting to your board, bring a female colleague who normally wouldn't attend but would benefit from observing the meeting. Not only will this raise her visibility with the board and company executives, but it will provide her firsthand insights into their thinking and decision-making process, thus facilitating her professional growth and knowledge. Alternatively, consider bringing a female colleague to executive team or cross-organizational project meetings. No matter the type of meeting, the key is to strategically think of whom to invite and why. Don't invite another woman leader just to do it. Invite her because it would benefit her professionally and personally, making it a value-added outcome. Make sure to let the meeting organizer know ahead of time that you're bringing along a female colleague and why. Describe how she'll benefit, as well as how the organization will benefit. Give your reasoning teeth by tying it to her professional development and the organization's business strategy.

SHARING THE SPOTLIGHT. There is a brilliant keynote speaker who is at the top of her game. She's a firm believer in amplification and practices it with enthusiasm—so much so that when asked to speak or be a panelist, she sometimes recommends another woman. She knows that being in front of an audience gives women incredible exposure that can lead to new opportunities and enhanced credibility. While she's an expert in her field, she understands there are plenty of other women with stellar credentials and there's no reason to hoard the spotlight. "I believe in the power of abundance," she says with a smile and a brightness in her eyes. "There's plenty to go around. If I can amplify another woman by giving up a speaking spot or being a panelist, I'm happy to do it." The next time you're offered a spotlight opportunity, such as a speaking engagement, consider elevating another qualified woman in your place or as a fellow panelist. While this may not always be the best option, asking yourself the question keeps your amplification muscle strong.

ROUTINE MEETINGS. During the course of your regular meetings, look for ways to amplify other women, such as publicly thanking or acknowledging them for their efforts. Point out how another woman led to the success of a project or the reaching of a milestone or how she resolved a sticking point or overcame a hurdle. In addition to verbal recognition, encourage women to physically sit in a prominent place in the room. As you read about in previous chapters, encourage her to refrain from sitting in a chair at the perimeter of the room and instead sit at the conference room table. You can take this a step further by arriving early to save a seat for her.

RECOMMEND AND ENDORSE. Keep attuned to promotions, lateral opportunities, and special projects for which you can recommend a woman. When such opportunities arise, recommend a talented woman to your boss or the decision maker. Advocate for and endorse her by sharing the expertise she brings to the table and how it can be leveraged further in a new role. Another angle is to encourage women to apply for promotions or lateral moves. Sometimes an encouraging nudge can prompt a woman to consider an opportunity she might have otherwise overlooked. Point out the ways her expertise, skills, and temperament align with the role. Additionally, as suggested in a 2021 *Fast Company* article, tell her to focus on three things: the responsibilities, the company or product, and the team. If those line up, then encourage her to go for it.

Collaboration over Competition

Competition may get you ahead based on your singular efforts, but collaboration will buoy you forward while in the company of supportive women who invest in each other. Podcasters and authors Aminatou Sow and Ann Friedman coined the term "Shine Theory" to describe "a practice of mutual investment with the simple premise that 'I don't shine if you don't shine'... [It's] a commitment to collaborating rather than competing against other people, especially other women."

The notion that women compete against one another rather than support one another is a long-standing stereotype about female professionals. I think it's time to shake that off in favor of collaboration. Imagine what women can achieve (and in fact have) through enhanced cooperation, collaboration, and amplification. We're fortunate to live in a time when numerous organizations exist that promote these ideals. LeanIn, Chief, and Women Together are a few organizations dedicated to championing women. As growing, effective communities, they recognize and nurture women's capabilities, ignite deep connections among women, and create lasting, positive change. This is inspiring and crucial for healthy work environments where women rely on one another in authentic ways that are generative. It requires mindset and behavioral shifts away from stereotypes of female competition to the narrative of collaboration and amplification. This doesn't have to start at the top. It starts with you and me. With *us*. The power of this shift has the capacity to ripple out to other women and eventually to organizational and societal structures.

Professional long-distance runner Shalane Flanagan is a prime example of someone who shattered stereotypes of female competition. She is a highly decorated runner, four-time Olympian, and in 2017 became the first American woman to win the New York City marathon in forty years. Complementing her extraordinary athletic achievements is her commitment to nurturing and encouraging the rising talent of other female distance runners. A 2017 *New York Times* opinion piece by Lindsay Crouse describes how Flanagan joined the Bowerman Track Club, where legendary distance coach Jerry Schumacher resides. At the time the article was written, Flanagan was the team's only woman. She worked with Schumacher to "create something new; a team of professional female distance runners who would train together and push one another to striking collective success."

While running is generally seen as an individual sport, Flanagan's commitment to advancing other women runners illustrates that you can be in a competitive field and still amplify others. Flanagan told Crouse, "I thoroughly enjoy working with other women. I think it makes me a better athlete and person. It allows me to have more passion toward my training and racing. When we achieve great things on our own, it doesn't feel as special." Crouse goes on to explain that Flanagan "brought in more women [to the club], elevating them to her level until they became the most formidable group of distance athletes in the nation. National championships, world championships, Olympics: They became some of the best runners in the world."

The individual success yet collaborative spirit of Flanagan's story stands as a reminder that women can be their best without sacrificing collaboration and mutual support. If you work in a competitive field, take note of Flanagan's story. What can you learn from it and apply in your own life? Take it upon yourself to write a new and better narrative for women. You have the ability to make a big difference in your field, just as Flanagan did.

Flanagan's story also reminds us of what it means to act from a place of abundance rather than scarcity. Operating from scarcity means there's only so much to go around so you better grab what you can before anyone else does. It means having a sense of lack based on the view of limited resources and opportunities. On the other hand, abundance means there's plenty for everyone. It's about seeing resources and opportunities as generative. Like Collaborative Confidence, an abundance mindset means deliberately investing in yourself and others, knowing that everyone benefits. Collaborative Confidence also creates an atmosphere where trust prevails, making women feel safe to share ideas and opportunities with each other, knowing they are in it together. The close connections with other women that stem from Collaborative Confidence is a natural platform that cultivates and grows an abundance mindset. The more you practice Collaborative Confidence, the stronger your abundance mindset becomes.

Another way to build an abundance mindset is to be intentional in your reaction and approach to challenges. Ask yourself, *What can I learn from this problem? How can I make this situation better? Who else can I involve in my problem-solving efforts?* These kinds of broad-thinking questions prompt discovery and creative solutions. They help move you forward in the midst of difficulty, opening up new possibilities. Scarcity thinking only keeps you stuck with thoughts such as, *Why does this always happen to me? This is never going to get better. There's no way to fix this, so I better just put up with it.* That kind of thinking keeps you trapped and isolated. Every time you catch yourself thinking a scarcity thought (*I shouldn't share credit. I'm never going to solve X. I better not tell so-and-so about this opportunity or I might lose it myself*), stop yourself and replace your thoughts with abundance (*Everyone deserves credit and there's plenty to go around. With resourcefulness and support, I bet I can solve X. It's tough right now, but I'm learning from the situation and trying to make it better*). This is the same principle as the name-notice-replace concept you read about in chapter 2.

Finally, another tactic to build your abundance mindset is to tune in to your inner champion and tune out your inner critic. Take nods from what you learned in chapter 2 and put them into practice. For instance, engage any of your five senses, including controlled breathing, sense of touch, and mindful eating and drinking. Or send a purposeful invitation to your inner champion asking her to remind you to be abundant in your thinking and actions. By using these tools and engaging in Collaborative Confidence, you'll strengthen your abundance mindset.

Abundance thinking leads you to positive, inspired action rather than destructive, entrenched behaviors. Perhaps it was inspired action that propelled Flanagan to create a female distance runners club upon her arrival at the Bowerman Track Club. Think of what you can do today to spark your own inspired action.

Amplifying other women, while they do the same for you, is at the heart of Collaborative Confidence. Commit to it today. Tell other women about Shine Theory. Share the story of the Obama administration, as well as Flanagan's, with other women. Let these agents of change inspire you. Together with other women, decide how you want to put amplification into action. Use what you learned in this chapter as your guide. Remember the significant ripple effects amplification can have for you and other women. Think of what you can do today to amplify other women. Create genuine, deep connections with other professional women and be committed to each other. Build a strong foundation where a healthy, inclusive work environment can grow and thrive.

SECTION III

Accelerate
DRIVE ESSENTIAL CHANGE

Organizations that strategically nurture the talents of women leaders and purposely create environments where they can truly thrive reap a multitude of benefits. It positively impacts the bottom line and creates a richer career pipeline for women leaders to traverse.

Chapter 8

Build Professional Environments Where Women Leaders Thrive

We've all heard the term "the glass ceiling" and associate it with the difficulties women face reaching the highest levels of leadership. However, long before a woman even gets a glimpse of the glass ceiling, she faces a difficult hurdle—"the broken rung." As described by McKinsey in their 2022 *Women in the Workplace* report, "Women continue to face a 'broken rung' at the first step up to manager: for every 100 men promoted to manager, only 86 women are promoted. As a result, men significantly outnumber women at the manager level, which means there are far fewer women promoted to higher levels." The broken rung is a persistent problem McKinsey first described in 2016, saying that it "makes it nearly impossible for companies to lay a foundation for sustained progress at more senior levels." Added to that, research by the Society of Human Resources Management (SHRM) paints a picture of how organizations risk losing top talent, especially women of color, when female leaders are overlooked. Their 2021 *Women in Leadership* report reveals that 21 percent of women leaders of color have quit a job after being overlooked for a new leadership role.

There are some glimmers of hope. According to McKinsey's report, women's representation across most of the corporate landscape has improved: "This year, for the first time, women of color were promoted to manager at about the same rate as women overall: 85 women of color were promoted for every 100 men." Additionally, a 2019 report by the IBM Institute for Business Value titled *Women, Leadership, and the Priority Paradox* identifies a small set of organizations they refer to as "First Movers." These companies work diligently to shift their corporate cultures by making the advancement of women leaders a formal business priority. The report speaks to the traction that is gained by deliberately weaving women's leadership initiatives into the strategic fabric of an organization. A majority of First Movers report higher performance than their competition in profitability, revenue growth, innovation, and employee satisfaction: "While First Movers haven't achieved fully gender-balanced leadership yet they are further along than others. This is solid evidence that the solution is in plain sight—if organizations are willing to address the issue with urgency and rigor." Despite such impressive outcomes, the report finds that most companies do not prioritize the advancement of women, at least not formally: 67 percent of respondents encourage promoting more women into leadership positions but fall short of making it a business priority, and 12 percent admit that advancing women "isn't on their radar." While respondents say they are interested in promoting more women into leadership positions and may have well-intentioned programs, the report contends that "unless the advancement of women is elevated to a formal business priority, our findings indicate that the likelihood of companies seeing a marked improvement is negligible."

To create environments where women leaders can thrive and the broken rung is fixed, the horsepower of America's corporations is needed. If more companies start taking intentional, bold actions to shift corporate cultures and advance more women into all levels of leadership, positive change is accelerated. As McKinsey said in their *Women in the Workplace* report, "When women are respected and their contributions are valued, they are more likely to be happy in their jobs and to feel connected to their coworkers." So far, we have explored strategies women can use to activate their self-awareness and amplify their authentic talents. Now, we are turning the page and shifting our attention to explore the responsibility organizations hold to foster female leadership. It's a two-way street. To create sustained change, organizations must embrace their responsibility and commit to systemic and sustained action. In this chapter, we'll explore avenues that help women leaders thrive through sponsorship, flexible work environments, and inclusive workplaces.

Sponsorship Opportunities

The role of a sponsor is a unique, powerful relationship that is different than that of a role model, coach, or mentor. While those relationships are powerful and can help your career path, there are important differences. A role model exemplifies effective and inspirational behaviors that you aspire to cultivate. A role model may be a person you know or someone you have never met, such as a famous politician, celebrity, or business leader. A coach, on the other hand, acts as a partner who uses a thought-provoking and creative process to inspire you to achieve your potential. A coach asks powerful questions to help you determine the path you wish to take. Finally, a mentor is an experienced advisor who shares their knowledge, skills, and expertise with you. They give you advice and direction based on their seasoned experience. A sponsor plays a different role. They use their influence and professional stature to advocate for you, their protégé. Sponsors are senior leaders who have visibility in the inner workings of an organization and are savvy about the corporate landscape. As the research group Catalyst puts it, "A role model talks by example, a coach talks to you, a mentor talks with you, and a sponsor talks about you."

One strategy to get a sponsor to talk about you is positioning yourself as an expert. Being seen as someone who is the best of the best is a surefire way to get a sponsor to sing your praises. As described by Samantha Ross Saperstein, head of Women on the Move at JPMorgan Chase, in a 2022 *Time* blog post, "Women [who are experts] are sought out for their unique knowledge or capability. People they work with universally agree on their level of mastery and view them as leaders in their domain. Sponsors want to work with them because they're considered the best at what they do." Saperstein describes how former secretary of state Condoleezza Rice exemplifies this:

> Rice's expertise in Soviet affairs gained the attention of former national security advisor Brent Scowcroft, who brought her to the White House and championed her as a valuable resource (as did both Bush presidents).

> Rice has shared with the Women on the Move community that President George H.W. Bush introduced her to Mikhail Gorbachev as his Soviet specialist who advised him on everything he needed to know about the Soviet Union. He didn't say that for Gorbachev's benefit, she explained; rather, he was signaling his support for her to everyone else around them. His message, as Rice recalled it, was, "That's my specialist, don't you dare try to tune her out."

Trust and respect are at the foundation of a sponsor-protégé relationship. It's born from a senior leader using their influence and corporate capital to advocate for a high-potential employee. For their part, the protégé shows they are committed, engaged, and results oriented. A sponsor opens doors and advocates on behalf of their protégé. They keep their protégé top-of-mind for promising opportunities and challenging assignments. They connect their protégé with their network of internal and external stakeholders, giving them opportunities to cultivate important relationships with influential, senior-level individuals. Sponsors also encourage their protégé to pursue roles, such as jobs with profit-and-loss responsibilities, to position them well for an eventual C-suite job.

WHY SPONSORSHIP MATTERS

The evidence about why a sponsor is important is clear. A 2020 co-authored report by Semi and Accenture, *Sponsorship of Women Drives Innovation and Improves Organizational Performance,* finds

- 38 percent of sponsored women vs. 30 percent of unsponsored women will ask for a raise;
- 44 percent of sponsored women vs. 36 percent of unsponsored women will ask for high-visibility work;
- and 68 percent of sponsored women vs. 57 percent of unsponsored women report satisfactory pace of promotions.

Adding to the data is the impact a sponsor has on pay. Research by Payscale reveals "those who have a sponsor are paid 11.6 percent more than those who do not. For men, the sponsorship premium is even higher: 12.3 percent. For women it is 10.2 percent." Furthermore, Payscale reports, "Hispanic women with a sponsor earn 6.1 percent more than Hispanic women without one. Black women with a sponsor earn 5.1 percent more than Black women without one." Pay is only one benefit you can reap from having a sponsor. Research by economist, author, and founder of Coqual (formerly the Center for Talent Innovation) Sylvia Ann Hewlett finds that entry-level employees with a sponsor are significantly more likely to get a stretch assignment. This is important because stretch assignments position you for upward career mobility and by their very nature broaden your thinking and organizational perspective.

Interestingly, sponsors themselves benefit from sponsorship. A 2019 *Harvard Business Review* article by Rania H. Anderson and David G. Smith says, "[Sponsors] are not benevolent benefactors. They are influential leaders who intentionally invest in, and rely on, the skills and contributions of their protégés to achieve their own goals and their protégés highest potential." Similarly, Hewlett, in a 2019 *Harvard Business Review* article, says, "Data shows that the sponsor. . . gains enormous values from [the] relationship." She goes on to point out that senior-level managers with a protégé are 53 percent more likely to have been promoted in the previous two years, and entry-level managers with a protégé are 60 percent more likely to get a stretch assignment. Sponsors also fare well when it comes to job satisfaction, with Hewlett's research indicating that 39 percent of sponsors with a protégé report "satisfaction with their professional legacies" while only 25 percent without a protégé say the same.

HOW TO FIND A SPONSOR

The data are clear: having a sponsor matters. Your company may not give you one, but that shouldn't stop you from seeking one out. Keep several things in mind on your quest to find a sponsor. The first is to be strategic. Identify a leader who is influential, is respected, and has their pulse on company initiatives. This may be your direct manager or someone above them in the reporting line. Interestingly, research by Payscale shows, "Nearly three-quarters of all respondents who say they have an advocate say that their direct manager is their sponsor, while an additional 16.3 percent of protégés said that their manager's manager was their sponsor. Only 10.5 percent said it was someone outside their department."

Regardless of who the potential sponsor is in relation to you on the organizational chart, having a sponsor is not a gift, it's something you earn. Strive to lay the groundwork to get the attention of a would-be sponsor. According to Hewlett, sponsors look for three things in a protégé: performance, trustworthiness, and commitment. Seek out and capitalize on opportunities to genuinely demonstrate these behaviors, as well as your own unique talents and strengths. Leverage the strategies you learned in chapter 6 to showcase your leadership, including reframing self-promotion as clear communication; seeing yourself as a role model for other women when you highlight your achievements; and raising your visibility through accentuating your physical presence, artfully claiming credit, speaking up, and skillfully managing interruptions. You may be fortunate to work in a company where sponsors are the norm. If that's not the case, getting a sponsor often occurs organically through relationship building.

Emma, a senior regional vice president at a retail chain, was a floor supervisor when she met Madeleine, who would later become her sponsor. During those early years, Emma established a trusting work relationship with Madeleine, who was her manager at the time. Emma loved her job and could see herself moving up in the organization. Thinking back to those early days when she was a floor supervisor, Emma shares, "I loved the fast-paced environment. It was invigorating, and every day was different. Even now as a VP that's still true, which is something I still love about my work. Back then, I loved the challenges of working in the store because it's a seven-days-of-the-week operation and that really kept me on my toes, especially since I was early in my career." She also recalls her affinity for working with customers. "I really enjoyed the customers and made it a point to establish a friendly rapport with them. I remember around the holidays it wasn't unusual for some of them to bring me a card or small gift. It was very sweet." She didn't even mind dealing with difficult customers because she saw it as a challenge. Thinking back on those early years, she believes it was a combination of her performance, commitment, trustworthiness, and friendly demeanor that caught Madeleine's attention.

Madeleine relied on Emma to understand the daily operations of the store, including recommendations to improve the customer experience, manage inventory needs, and motivate employees. Emma freely shared her ideas and other important knowledge she gained from being on the store floor with Madeleine. She also routinely asked Madeleine what she could do for her and how she could help Madeleine with her own critical, pressing priorities. All of these behaviors imprinted on Madeleine Emma's drive and commitment. They also shared a natural, friendly rapport, which made working together enjoyable. While Emma did not intentionally set out to find a sponsor, the personal behaviors she exhibited—coupled with her outstanding performance, talents, and strengths—set the opportunity in motion. Madeleine used her influence and corporate capital to advocate for Emma. She introduced Emma to other senior leaders and spoke highly of her at leadership team meetings. She assigned special projects to Emma, sent her to professional conferences, and publicly endorsed her in front of other stakeholders. She also recommended Emma for stretch assignments and promotions. Emma recalls one particular stretch assignment in which she led a multistore cost-savings initiative that required intense financial analysis. "At first I was nervous about it and frankly intimidated," says Emma. "It was an important project with a lot of visibility. I led a task force that was hand-selected by the executive time, and we had some pretty tight deliverables. I also had to regularly travel to the corporate office to make presentations and give recommendations to our executive team. And they were known for being a tough audience." While leading the project initially made her nervous, Madeleine gave Emma all the tools and resources to be successful, including being a sounding board along the way. "I really appreciated the support and guidance Madeleine gave me. She also empowered me and gave me the latitude to run the project with sufficient autonomy that stretched me professionally." Today, Emma credits Madeleine's sponsorship as the key reason behind her rise from floor supervisor to senior regional vice president, covering a large geographic territory across the mid-Atlantic states.

While for Emma and Madeleine sponsorship developed through work-related activities, other times mutual interests pave the way. Sharing personal interests can lay the groundwork for a would-be sponsor to learn more about you on an individual level and telegraph appealing leadership and work-related qualities. Mutual interests can illuminate your values, principles, and other intrinsic qualities that a would-be sponsor might associate with success. They might pick up on your knack for creative problem-solving, skilled diplomacy, comfort with risk-taking, or competitive spirit, for example. They might also get a solid understanding of your reliability, trustworthiness, and loyalty. As illustrated by Condoleezza Rice's story, positioning yourself as an expert is another strategy to catch the attention of a potential sponsor. Consider your expertise, whether it be technical skills, negotiation acumen, strategic forecasting, skilled diplomacy, or something else. Look for opportunities to demonstrate your expertise as a way to make your mark as well as get noticed by a potential sponsor.

SPONSORSHIP ROADBLOCKS

Clearly, research shows that women who have a sponsor are afforded more opportunities in both their roles and pay. Sadly, however, in a 2019 *Harvard Business Review* article, professor and author Herminia Ibarra says, "Too few women are reaching the top of their organizations and a big reason is that they are not getting the high-stakes assignments that are prerequisite for a shot at the C-suite. Often, this is due to a lack of powerful sponsors demanding and ensuring that they get these stepping-stone jobs." Ibarra goes on to say that "women tend to be over-mentored and under-sponsored." Similarly, McKinsey's 2019 report *Taking the Lead for Inclusion* indicates "34 percent of women feel they don't have equal access to sponsorship." Coupled with that is research by Payscale showing the racial disparity between white men and women of color when it comes to having a sponsor. Their research reveals that 62.5 percent of white men report having a sponsor in comparison to 55 percent of Black and Hispanic women.

The reason women are not sponsored at the same rate as men may be explained by gender. According to Payscale, "Protégés gender is typically the same as their sponsor." Men outnumber women in leadership positions, as pointed out in 2018 article by *Scientific American* saying, "Only 28 percent of American CEOs are women." At the management level, research group Catalyst finds 40.9 percent of managers in 2021 were women. The fact that there are more men in leadership positions coupled with research that there's usually a gender match between protégé and sponsor helps explain why women have less access to sponsors. Race and ethnicity follow a similar vein according to Paycale's research: "Over 90 percent of white men and women protégés who reported the race/ethnicity of their sponsor said that they were also white. Women protégés of other racial/ethnic groups were far less likely to report that their sponsor was white. Just over half of Black and Hispanic women protégés reported having white sponsors: 58.8 percent and 59.4 percent, respectively."

SPONSORSHIP AND ORGANIZATIONAL CULTURE

Sponsorship does not rest solely on the shoulders of individual women. To build environments where women leaders thrive, organizations bear responsibility. Weaving sponsorship into the fabric of a company's culture is at the heart of lasting, systematic, inclusive change. This may include tying sponsorship to organizational KPI's (key performance indicators) or the company's talent strategy. Companies that commit to inclusive organizational environments where sponsorship programs are imbedded into the culture create systematic change. This characterizes the kind of workplace where great talent wants to work.

It all starts at the top. Executive leaders who thoughtfully and strategically institute a well-designed sponsorship program create a diverse talent pipeline that creates a pathway to top-level jobs. Company performance benefits from cultivating a diverse culture and leadership team. Research compiled by Catalyst in their 2020 *Why Diversity and Inclusion Matter: Financial Performance* report reveals a correlation between leader diversity and positive financial performance including profitability, gross and net margins, and revenue. In their 2019 *Harvard Business Review* article, Anderson and Smith concur, saying, "If companies truly want to improve their financial results and diversity, they need to do a better job of developing sponsors for diverse talent at all levels of their organization. Leaders are regularly taught about strategic thinking, championing change, making financial decisions, and managing people, but they are not taught how to become sponsors or maximize their impact in the role." In addition, Anderson and Smith go on to say, "Gender balance in companies and on teams improves a host of outcomes including financial results, innovation, decision-making, organizational commitment, retention and job satisfaction."

Before creating a sponsorship program, companies would do well to do their homework. Trying to achieve a quick fix with a hastily crafted program is likely to be met with resistance and be ineffective. Designing and instituting an effective program includes several deliberate steps, such as the ones listed below.

Weave Sponsorship into the Culture

Buy-in and endorsement from an organization's entire leadership team is key to weaving sponsorship into a company's culture. Tying the program to organizational priorities and goals as well as establishing metrics and milestones helps give the program teeth.

Organizations can track promotions, lateral moves, and retention rates, for example. This data can then be used to demonstrate the financial benefits reaped by the company as well as the benefits to protégés and sponsors.

Clearly Define Roles

Just because a sponsor is a senior leader does not necessarily mean they know how to be an effective sponsor. Being in a sponsor-protégé relationship includes consistently checking in, demonstrating commitment, and having frank conversations. In addition, the sponsor provides direction, offers different perspectives, advocates for the protégé, gives direct and candid feedback, and assigns stretch assignments that drive the business forward while elevating the protégé's visibility. The protégé takes on increasingly important work while delivering results, demonstrating loyalty, and keeping their sponsor apprised of critical developments.

Identify High-Potential Talent

A protégé is a valued employee whose ambition, talent, and potential position them to make an even larger contribution to the organization. There are numerous ways to identify high-potential employees: strong job performance, personal aspiration to rise in the organization, track record of fostering positive relationships with colleagues, and drive to take on more complex and visible responsibilities.

Identify Stretch Roles

For the success of the protégé and benefit to both the sponsor and organization, it's wise to identify high-visibility stretch roles that capitalize on the protégé's talents and generate meaningful business results. According to Anderson and Smith's 2019 *Harvard Business Review* article, "The best opportunities to develop protégés are those that meet some of these conditions: involves profit and loss; high risk; strategic clients; importance to the business; starting something new; or fixing a business problem."

Provide Structure and Support

The structure of a stretch assignment needs to be clearly articulated so the protégé knows what is expected of them, including responsibilities, time frame, and resources to which they'll have access. Additionally, its incumbent upon the sponsor to convey how the assignment fits into the broader organizational context and how the protégé will benefit from stepping into the role. The sponsor should also be candid about the support and feedback they'll give the protégé along the way and what the protégé can expect from them. This may include regular meetings to discuss the progress of the stretch assignment as well as provide support on how to navigate obstacles and work with new senior leaders.

Taking comprehensive steps that are thought through and executed with care is foundational to creating an effective sponsorship program. Organizations that commit to embedding sponsorship into the fabric of their company benefit all the way around. This includes improved financial results, longer employee retention, and enhanced job satisfaction. Moreover, sponsorships afford greater upward mobility for women leaders and may help organizations address the broken-rung problem.

Minimize Burnout

The chief human resources officer (CHRO) of a marketing firm had been keeping her eye on the toll the COVID-19 pandemic was taking on the company's employees. Burnout was nothing new for this fast-paced work environment where meeting client demands was paramount. Before the pandemic the CHRO hadn't given much attention to the idea of burnout, but that began to change during the first half of 2020. As she talked with colleagues at other companies, listened to podcasts, and read business articles, it became clear that burnout is more than stress. As pointed out by the consulting firm DDI, "Stress can cause you to feel disheartened or frustrated, but can be improved by slowing down, problem solving or taking a vacation. Burnout, however, is the feeling of chronic, unrelenting stress accompanied by intense negative feelings such as hopeless, exhaustion and disillusionment. Motivation dries up and obstacles may feel insurmountable." This was a revelation to the CHRO, who came to understand that what she once chalked up as stress among their employees was actually burnout.

Burnout can arise in subtle ways, creeping in so quietly you may not notice it at first. Low energy becomes exhaustion, sleeplessness becomes insomnia, impatience becomes irritability, an occasional short fuse becomes prolonged anger, and disinterest with work becomes apathy. It's a miserable way to live. For companies, burnout creates fatigued employees, which adversely impacts performance and productivity. Exhausted employees may even decide to quit and take their experience, knowledge, and intellectual capital with them. According to LeanIn.Org and McKinsey's 2022 *Women in the Workplace* report, the risk of companies losing female leaders is higher than male leaders: "Women are even more burned out now than they were a year ago, and the gap in burnout between women and men has almost doubled. In the past year, one in three women has considered leaving the workforce or downshifting their career, a significant increase from one in four in the first few months of the pandemic."

The marketing firm's CHRO became increasingly alarmed about the impact of burnout on the company's employees as well as the organization itself. She understood how burnout could further adversely impact employees and in turn erode the business. Knowing that addressing burnout comes from the top and requires systematic change, she met with the firm's executive team and shared a number of data points, including Gallup's 2020 *Perspective on Employee Burnout: Causes and Cures* report. It reveals that employees who say they always or very often experience burnout at work are

- 63 percent more likely to take a sick day;
- 23 percent more likely to visit an emergency room;
- 2.6 times more likely to actively seek another job;
- and 3 percent less confident in their performance.

The CHRO also shared Gallup's finding that employees who experience burnout are only half as likely to discuss how to address performance expectations with their manager. These employees, according to Gallup, resist coaching and have a mindset fixated on problems rather than solutions and success. Thankfully, the executive team understood the looming burnout crisis they were facing and took immediate action. Their first move was to establish a cross-organizational working group to address burnout. The group was made up of staff from various levels and departments and was charged with making recommendations to the executive team. The group made a number of recommendations that the firm adopted, including the following:

> **BOUNDARY SETTING.** A flexible work environment where remote work is the norm gives employees freedom and independence, but it also blurs the lines between home life and work life. Without clear boundaries, employees working with a flexible schedule may perceive they are always "on." McKinsey's 2022 *Women in the Workplace* report says of their research of 65,000 survey respondents from 423 participating organizations, "More than a third of employees feel like they need to be available for work 24/7, and almost half believe they need to work long hours to get ahead." While employees should feel they have the authority to shut down for the day, companies have a responsibility to set boundaries around work time as well as more clearly define performance expectations. The CHRO shared with the executive team that the McKinsey report also says, "Only one in five employees says that their company has told

them that they don't need to respond to nonurgent requests outside of traditional work hours, and only one in three has received guidance around blocking off personal time on their calendar." It was clear that the marketing firm needed to take action to establish work norms. So, they turned to the cross-functional working group and asked them to come back with recommendations. The group's ideas included establishing core work hours from 9:00 a.m. to 3:30 p.m. when employees are available for collaboration, meetings, and communication; eliminating late-night and weekend emails; and shortening one-hour meetings by ten minutes so employees have a break before their next one. A creative recommendation was to offer noontime stretch breaks, where employees can gather (virtually or in-person) for fifteen minutes of stretching to relieve muscle tension and promote relaxation.

MANAGEABLE WORKLOAD. Juggling a demanding workload, managing competing priorities, and working long hours is a common experience among employees. According to a 2020 Gallup post, the number of hours worked in a week is associated with burnout. They report the risk of burnout dramatically increases when employees exceed fifty hours a week and climbs even more after sixty hours. When a person's workload seems consistently endless and burdensome, it can feel like you're drowning and it's hard to come up for air. The cross-organizational working group recommended the firm do a workforce analysis review to assess projects and priorities against staffing levels. They also recommended the review include taking a hard look at projects that could be delayed or eliminated altogether, as well as if hiring more staff was needed.

ENHANCED PERFORMANCE REVIEWS. When work is performed in-person, it allows managers and employees many more opportunities to interface and engage with each other than in a remote work environment. From planned meetings to impromptu hallway conversations to seeing each other in the cafeteria, sharing the same physical space affords all kinds of interaction opportunities. The accumulation of such interactions lets managers see employees in a cross-section of activities, giving the manager a full picture of observable behaviors. This is more difficult, if not impossible, when work is performed remotely. To level the playing field, the cross-organizational working group recommended a number of changes to the firm's performance-appraisal system: First, to incorporate peer feedback to give managers a fuller performance picture of their direct reports. Second, to add a self-evaluation component so each employee could assess themselves and provide their perspective of their performance and contributions. The group found this particularly important. As professors Bret Sanner and Karoline Evans discuss in a 2021 *Harvard Business Review* article, employees generally overestimate the degree their accomplishments are noticed and remembered. To mitigate this, a self-evaluation is an important tool employees can use to highlight their accomplishments and bring them to the forefront of their manager's mind. Finally, the working group recommended revising the goal-setting section of the firm's performance-appraisal form. The group suggested incorporating the firm's corporate values as well as the employee's. This would give each employee and their manager an opportunity to better understand what was intrinsically important to an employee.

Another critical element of reducing burnout is the role of managers and leaders. Managers in particular are on the front lines of an employee's workday, giving them multiple opportunities to engage, observe, and check in with their team members. The firm held training sessions to support and equip them. It included a formal training program as well as biweekly virtual lunch n' learn sessions.

The training program included educating managers and leaders on the topic of burnout as well as signs to watch for among their employees, including disengagement, loss of motivation, reduced performance, chronic exhaustion, trouble concentrating, difficulty learning, and prolonged irritability. The training program also conveyed the important role managers play. They learned that, according to a 2021 *Harvard Business Review* article by Tiffany Burns, Jess Huang, Alexis Krivkovich, Ishanaa Rambachan, Tijana Trkulja, and Lareina Yee, "when managers actively managed the workload of their team, their staff were 32 percent less likely to be burned out and 33 percent less likely to leave." From that same article, the managers learned that "when managers support employee well-being, employees are 25 percent more likely to be happy at work." Because of this and other research, the training program centered on the following important skills: empathy, listening, soliciting opinions, and communicating clearly.

SHOW EMPATHY. Managing with empathy means having the ability to understand and care about the needs of one's direct reports and being aware of their thoughts and feelings. According to research by Catalyst, "Empathy is an important driver of employee outcomes such as innovation, engagement, and inclusion—especially in times of crisis." Catalyst also finds that employees experience less burnout when their managers are empathetic, and this is especially true for women of color. Furthermore, having an empathetic leader significantly increases a woman's intention to stay at her job. Catalyst's research also shows that when employees experience empathy from their leader, they are better able to balance work obligations with personal ones. The marketing firm's training program included how to genuinely connect with direct reports in a way that demonstrates care and concern. It also included the importance of acknowledging difficulties an employee may be facing. The leaders learned that empathy can cultivate connections with employees that generate positive, intrinsic feelings while supporting the employee's capacity to innovate, flourish, and perform at work. The training program covered a number of skills, including sincerely asking employees about their feelings and reflecting back what was heard; getting to know employees on a more personal basis including hobbies, interest, and family; and listening with full attention.

LISTEN EFFECTIVELY. While the idea of listening may not seem particularly novel, in their 2020 *Employee Burnout: Causes and Cures* report, Gallup finds, "Employees whose manager is always willing to listen to their work-related problems are 62 percent less likely to be burned out. To help combat burnout, employees need to believe that their manager will address their problems, and they need to feel like their manager genuinely cares about them as people." The firm's manager training program incorporated a number of listening strategies you read about in chapter 5, including the power of pausing and 360-degree listening. In the training program, the managers learned the undeniable power genuine listening has to make employees feel heard, respected, and appreciated.

SOLICIT OPINIONS. According to Gallup's *Employee Burnout: Causes and Cures* report, "When employees believe their opinions are welcome and make a difference, they feel important and included, and they begin taking more responsibility for their performance. This sense of ownership reduces burnout because it gives employees a feeling of control over their work—rather than feeling like work is something that happens to them." The training program encourages managers to solicit their employees' ideas and opinions formally and informally. Formally includes during one-on-one sessions, while informally includes quick emails or phone calls to an employee asking for their opinion on something. Managers are encouraged to initiate open, genuine dialogue to mine for and collaborate on ideas. An important action is managers following up with employees so they know the outcome of their ideas.

COMMUNICATE CLEARLY. When managers regularly communicate and provide ongoing information, employees feel knowledgeable and equipped to do their job. When that doesn't happen, it can be a source of frustration that can contribute to fatigue and foster burnout. Communicating clearly and frequently is especially important in a virtual environment. The firm's training program emphasized the importance of conveying responsibilities, expectations, goals, priorities, and the like. The program also highlighted that communication is not a one-way street. It is not a lecture where the manager does all of the talking. Instead, it's a dialogue that includes the manager asking questions, soliciting input, clarifying information, and encouraging the employee to talk.

In addition to the training program that emphasized the above, leaders were invited to participate in monthly lunch n' learn sessions where they could hone their skills and reinforce their learning. The sessions included additional exercises, case studies, and information as well as peer coaching. There, leaders would coach each other on their own challenges, frustrations, and stress. This served as a supportive and empathetic outlet that helped them avoid burnout as they helped others avoid it, too.

As one leader put it, "I get a lot of value talking with my peers because I get ideas I never would have thought of on my own. And as a leader, there are so few people you can talk to and really share what's going on with you. So personally, this has been a great outlet for me."

Addressing burnout requires a systematic approach in which a company examines and tackles it from several angles. The adverse impact of burnout on employees, as well as organizations as a whole, is enormous and not worth the price. Addressing burnout begins with executive leadership setting the tone and taking tangible, active measures to alleviate it.

Foster Inclusivity

Feeling included is a basic human desire. We all want to be seen, acknowledged, and valued. And we all know what it feels like not to be. In my experience, inclusion generates collaborative and cohesive teams and makes work meaningful and enjoyable. A 2019 *Harvard Business Review* article by Karyn Twaronite describes, "When people feel like they belong at work, they are more productive, motivated, engaged and 3.5 times more likely to contribute to their fullest potential." SHRM's 2021 *Women in Leadership* report concurs about what inclusive cultures generate. Employees who consider inclusiveness at their workplace as excellent are "nearly two and a half times more likely to recommend their organization to others as a great place to work (90 percent versus 37 percent), and to feel respected and valued at work (92 percent versus 38 percent)." On the other side of the coin, Bain and Company's *The Fabric of Belonging: How to Weave an Inclusive Culture* 2022 report reveals that "women who feel excluded at work are three times more likely to quit than those who feel included." Clearly, all of this data creates a compelling reason to foster inclusive environments where women leaders thrive.

Inclusion is a complex subject with many nuanced facets, making it challenging for organizations to identify specific ways to promote it. However, research by Bain offers some direction, saying that people describe inclusion in similar ways. When asked what inclusion looks like, respondents agreed that "an inclusive organization is one that is diverse and in which people are heard, valued, and supported." When asked what it feels like, respondents said "it is being treated with dignity, able to bring their authentic selves to work, able to contribute, and feeling connected to others."

Naomi recalls starting at her current job where she is vice president of corporate communications for a hotel chain. What a refreshing change from where she previously worked. "Here, I feel genuinely included, respected, and supported. Even when I have a different opinion, people hear me out," she says. "At my last employer, a lot of times I was left out of meetings and decisions. It was very siloed. I felt like all they cared about was me hitting the numbers. My opinions and ideas weren't important. The focus was all about making money and not about how people were treated." Today, with a sparkle in her eye, Naomi talks about how respected she feels for her expertise, strengths, and opinions. Senior leaders rely on her wealth of knowledge and give her the autonomy to exercise it. She adds, "There's also a strong sense of mutual respect here. Employees all the way around, at every level, genuinely respect one another's expertise." The sense of inclusion Naomi feels has made an indelible mark on her. She can't imagine working anywhere else. Her story demonstrates that inclusive cultures foster engagement, satisfaction, and retention.

Another aspect of the organization culture at Naomi's job that made an immediate, positive imprint on her is the support and genuine concern she gets from other employees—superiors, peers, colleagues, and direct reports. "I've not felt this kind of genuine teamwork before. Don't get me wrong, it's not all roses and butterflies, but there is a strong sense of encouragement that permeates the organization. The hotel wants all of us to make meaningful contributions and have a sense of connection."

Naomi's experience is consistent with research by McKinsey that they describe in a 2021 blog post. It describes inclusion from two angles: personal experience, which includes authenticity, belonging, and meaningful work; and enterprise perception, which includes acceptance, camaraderie, and fairness. McKinsey goes on to point out that company policies are necessary but must be complemented with consistently meaningful behaviors from leaders, colleagues, and teams that make inclusion real.

Creating an inclusive work environment starts at the top and cascades down into the organization. Leaders set the tone as role models through their behaviors and establish policies and practices for the organization. Inclusion is not one thing; it's many things woven together that are consistently cultivated. Leaders can foster inclusion through such practices as participative decision-making, encouraging authentic self-expression, providing access to information and opportunities, offering bias-sensitivity training, instilling cooperation, demonstrating respect, and encouraging healthy conflict resolution focused on mutual learning and understanding. Organizations are encouraged to solicit employee feedback about instilling a culture of inclusion. After all, it will never be an inclusive culture if senior leaders take an isolated approach to create one. That's the exact opposite of inclusion. Soliciting feedback from employees on what makes them feel included and getting their ideas on meaningful steps to foster inclusion can be obtained several ways, including employee surveys, focus groups, and one-on-one interviews.

Organizations can create work environments where women leaders thrive by taking active steps to address the broken-rung problem. This can be accomplished through meaningful sponsorship opportunities, addressing burnout, and creating a culture of inclusion. It begins with top leadership making a commitment to focus on women's leadership and taking active measures to weave it into the entire culture. Not only do individual women benefit, but so do the organizations where they work, with improved financial performance, employee retention, and motivation. Organizations can be inspired by the stories of Emma and Naomi in their quest to cultivate work environments where women leaders can thrive.

Chapter 9

Cultivate More Human-Centric Corporate Cultures

When organizations say they put their people first, that means every process, business decision, and policy has a human-centric aspect to it. Putting people at the center of the business means valuing their input, developing their talents, and addressing problems that affect them. In my experience, creating a human-centric culture includes taking action on important matters such as a flexible work and equal pay. When women leaders endure inflexible work environments and pay inequity, companies are at risk of losing them. That's not good for women, and it's not good for business. Addressing these issues are two infrastructure strategies companies can use to foster a human-centric culture.

This should matter to companies, because when women are more equitably represented in leadership ranks, organizations benefit in several ways, including financially. Extensive research over a seventeen-year period (2002 to 2019) by S&P Global reveals attention-grabbing results in their *When Women Lead, Firms Win* report:

- Firms with female CFOs are more profitable.
- Firms with female CEOs and CFOs generate superior stock price performance in comparison to the market average.
- When there's higher gender diversity on the board of directors, the firm is more profitable.

S&P Global adds, "Over the time-horizon of the study, female CEOs saw more value appreciation and improved stock price momentum for their firms; whereas female CFOs drove more value appreciation, better defended profitability moats, and delivered excess risk adjusted returns for their firms."

Similar eye-opening analysis on gender in the C-suite comes from Quantopian, a Boston-based trading firm that compared returns from 2002 to 2014 of Fortune 1000 companies led by female CEOs to those of the S&P 500. Remarkably, Quantopian's research reveals that companies led by women saw returns that were 226 percent higher.

The mere fact of having more women in leadership doesn't automatically mean greater financial gains for organizations. A number of factors may be in play, including hiring from a diverse pool of job candidates, which may mean an organization is better positioned to find the best talent. Additionally, diversity among top leadership may spark more critical thinking, robust decision-making, and dynamic problem-solving.

The benefits of more women in leadership positions extends beyond the bottom line. As described by professors and researchers Corinne Post, Boris Lokshin, and Christophe Boone in a 2021 *Harvard Business Review* article, companies with more women in senior positions are more socially responsible, open to change, and interested in research and development strategies. The benefits of having women in top leadership positions is clear. By addressing flexible work and equal pay, organizations create environments that are human-centric, which is something that attracts and helps retain talented women leaders. Let's explore both.

Create a Flexible Work Environment

Flexibility in the workplace is another necessary component to addressing the broken-rung problem women leaders face. The COVID-19 pandemic illuminated not just the necessity for a flexible work environment but proved it can be effective. Companies scrambled at the beginning to keep their operations going by quickly assembling remote and hybrid work structures. Today, remote and hybrid work structures remain common. As reported in March 2022 by the *Wall Street Journal,* "A recent survey by the Labor Department found that more than a third of employers increased telework because of the pandemic, and 60.2 percent expect to keep the increases permanent when the pandemic is over." Flexible work schedules align companies and employees on business results and work-life needs.

Beyond the practicality of and desire for a flexible work structure that may include remote and hybrid work, there are signs it fosters employee well-being. LeanIn.Org and McKinsey's 2021 *Women in the Workplace* report states, "More than three quarters of senior HR leaders say allowing employees to work flexible hours is one of the most effective things they've done to improve employee well-being, and there are clear signs it's working. Employees with more flexibility to take time off and step away from work are much less likely to be burned out, and very few employees are concerned that requesting flexible work arrangements has impacted their opportunity to advance."

Each organization culture is unique, which makes embedding flexibility distinctive for every company. Michelle Nettles, chief people and culture officer at Milwaukee-based Manpower Group, told SHRM in March 2021, "We need to be more intentional about understanding what workers want, and especially what women want. Lack of flexible work, lack of role models, gendered career paths, and challenges accessing sponsors and influential networks were already holding women back."

Organizations are cautioned not to frame flexibility as a woman's issue, as that creates a stigma and only further embeds outdated gendered norms. As professors W. Brad Johnson and David G. Smith put it in their 2021 *Harvard Business Review* article, "Extending more flexible work arrangements to all workers, not just women, can disrupt the associated stigma by avoiding assumptions about who will want to use flexible work arrangements." A further caution relates to companies shifting their definition of what a valued worker looks like. Rather than it being someone who is in the office five days a week, a valued employee can just as easily be a person working a flexible, remote, or hybrid schedule.

Women already face an uneven playing field, as illustrated by the broken-rung hurdle and lack of sponsorship. To move ahead, women benefit from internal networks and influential stakeholders, which become all the more difficult to build and cultivate with a flexible, hybrid, or remote schedule where face-to-face time is reduced or eliminated altogether. Virtual meetings don't lend themselves to informal "do you have a minute?" hallway conversations, spontaneous networking, or in-the-moment decision-making. As you read in chapter 6, and have likely experienced yourself, women sometimes find it hard to speak up in meetings or to be heard when they do. This is compounded in a virtual work environment where it can be challenging to interject a comment or raise a concern. Research by Catalyst found that 45 percent of women leaders say it's difficult to speak up in virtual meetings and 25 percent report they've felt ignored or overlooked during video meetings. Their research also shows that three in five female employees believe their prospects of getting a promotion are worse in a remote work environment.

Organizations are cautioned not to allow a flexible, hybrid, or remote environment to exacerbate existing hurdles women already face. This is something Gloria, a senior vice president at a transportation and logistics company, was well aware of. As an avid reader, she was familiar with Johnson and Smith's *Harvard Business Review* article and the research from Catalyst. While she knew there are no perfect answers, she was convinced her company would do well to monitor and analyze promotions, stretch assignments, sponsorships, and other leadership development strategies for employees regardless of their work arrangement—in-person, hybrid, remote, or flexible schedule. As Gloria prepared to make her case to the executive team, she first consulted with the chief human resources officer (CHRO), who fully endorsed the idea. Next, she equipped herself with research and data. She also did a competitive analysis of other transportation and logistics companies and found that her organization could use a flexible work culture as a unique value proposition to attract and retain top talent. Because of her due diligence and reputation as a well-respected senior vice president, the executive team embraced her recommendations. The company now collects data related to promotions, stretch assignments, sponsorships, and other leadership development activities and compares it across different work arrangements.

Today, Gloria says, "We're able to quickly see trends and warning signs that might indicate disproportionately fewer opportunities for employees on a flexible, hybrid, or remote schedule. And we can see that for women and underrepresented employees, too. This kind of tracking and data helps us get ahead of potential problems so we can take action." But it's not only about the numbers, as Gloria explains.

"We try to paint as full a picture as possible. That means we also take into account performance metrics and other skill and talent indicators we used during pre-pandemic times to assess promotional and stretch assignment readiness. Job opportunities still need to be supported by performance regardless of the employee's work structure." These combined efforts make the company's flexible work schedule, promotions, stretch assignments, sponsorships, and leadership development activities a more even playing field for all.

Gloria was also aware that leading meetings (particularly virtual ones) needs to be done in an inclusive way where people, especially women, are able to comfortably speak up. Even at her high level, she experienced the challenges of speaking up, particularly in a virtual setting. Buoyed by the support she had previously received from the executive leadership team, she partnered again with the CHRO to instill this into the company culture, too. Today, she and the CHRO offer a series of lunch n' learn sessions for anyone in a supervisory position and above to train them on leading effective and inclusive virtual meetings. The sessions include content about thinking through who has been invited to a meeting and being mindful of casting the net wide enough so that all who should be included are. Participants learn this may mean taking the extra step of asking someone else (say, one of the meeting attendees), "Is there anyone else I should include?" The lunch n' learn participants also learn that during virtual meetings, they need to take extra steps to ensure everyone has the opportunity to fully participate in order to mitigate feelings of being ignored or overlooked. One tactic they learn is to pose a question, give meeting attendees a few minutes of quiet writing time to jot down their thoughts, and follow that by round-robin sharing. The sessions also include content on using technology to foster inclusion, such as the chat function, annotation tools, and electronic whiteboards.

Participants learn they can also ask meeting attendees to respond electronically to a question or idea and continue the discussion by asking follow-up questions, such as "Morgan, can you say more about your comment in the chat?" or "Casey, on the electronic whiteboard, you described the customer as old-fashioned. Can you say more?" Another tactic the participants learn is to open meetings by explicitly inviting everyone to participate. This includes letting attendees know that if multiple people start to talk at once, they'll make sure each person gets a chance to speak. Finally, another tactic they learn is to pose an opening and ending question that everyone is asked to answer, such as "What's the first word that comes to mind when you think of this project?" or "What is one question you want clarified today?" or "What is the first action you'll take based upon today's meeting?" or "What is one other piece of information you'd like to have?"

Gloria proudly shares the positive impact of their lunch n' learn sessions. "I've had employees come to me, on their own, telling me they finally feel included in meetings. It's so encouraging to hear them talk about being able to say something and have it actually paid attention to. I remember one employee telling me that before, she just endured virtual meetings, sitting there not saying a word, because every time she tried, she'd be interrupted. But now, it's totally different. Another employee told me that before the training, her manager used to talk all throughout virtual meetings like it was a monologue or lecture. But now, he asks a lot of questions, encourages people to talk, and makes people feel included."

Creating a Flexible Work Structure

To weave various flexible work structures into the fabric of organization culture, companies are encouraged to take a collaborative approach that includes input from employees. Understanding the collective preferences, needs, and expectations of the workforce and incorporating that input into work schedule policies makes employees feel heard and included. While work structures are unique to each organization's culture, considerations include the following:

> **WORK LOCATION.** By the nature of the work itself, some jobs are not suited for remote work, such as a grocery store manager, emergency room doctor, or television field reporter. Other work can be accomplished remotely, especially with the popularity of various video conference technologies, software systems, and team collaboration platforms. Even jobs in finance, law, consulting, and engineering, which once demanded in-person meetings and travel, are now conducive to remote work.

> **WORK HOURS.** I recall my first corporate job, where we were expected, with no exceptions, to be at our desks working by 7:30 a.m. and not leave for home until the clock struck 4:30 p.m. In more recent years, and especially since the pandemic, flexible work hours are more standard. This may apply to the number of hours worked in a day or working from home some days. This acceptance recognizes employees are capable of getting their work done while working flexible hours or days.

> **HYBRID WORK.** A work arrangement that gained enormous traction as a result of the pandemic is

hybrid work, where an employee works a portion of their week in the office and the rest from home. It offers employees flexibility while reducing operational costs. In some work environments, the in-office days are standard for all, while in others, the in-office days are staggered among the staff. Each company culture is different, so a hybrid work structure should align with it.

The CHRO at a private college led workforce and people strategies throughout the COVID-19 pandemic. As the pandemic progressed, it became more evident that flexible work policies and structures needed to be put in place. The CHRO, along with the entire executive team, understood that the college needed to weave flexibility into the fabric of its culture to meet the changing way work is performed.

A cross-functional task force was created to tackle the challenge. It included administrators, staff, and faculty from all levels of the university. The executive team understood that undertaking such a large organizational change meant doing it collaboratively. The cross-functional team engaged in several activities, including the following:

EMPLOYEE INPUT. The team gathered feedback, ideas, and input through employee surveys and focus groups. This allowed them to learn and take into consideration various perspectives, as well as assess the suitability of various flexible work arrangements for the university. This step in their strategy also planted the seed for buy-in early on and continued throughout the duration of their work.

VIRTUAL TOWN HALL MEETINGS. On a regular cadence, the team hosted virtual town hall meetings where they provided updates on their work and answered questions. They also presented research on the benefits of a flexible work schedule as a way of neutralizing the notion that it's a women's issue.

COMMUNICATION CHANNELS. The team established an electronic portal for employees to anonymously ask questions and give suggestions. The portal also included updates from the task force as well as recorded messages from the college president, CHRO, and members of the cross-functional team.

POLICIES AND PROCEDURES. Clear policies and procedures are an important step in instituting organizational change. The cross-functional team drafted an initial set of flexible workplace policies and procedures and presented them to the human resources advisory team, which was an existing committee charged with evaluating human resources policies and procedures. After their input was incorporated and their recommendation for adoption was received, the policies and procedures were presented to the college's executive leadership team for final approval. The policies and procedures were then posted on the college's internal website and communicated through virtual town hall meetings.

MANAGER AND EMPLOYEE TRAINING. The cross-functional team led various training sessions so managers and employees understood what the college's new flexible work environment was all about. The training included going over the new policies and procedures. The training sessions also conveyed that performance is based on results and outcomes, not time in the office. A member of the cross-functional team shares, "We were well aware of the possible bias toward employees who work in-person over those who work remotely. We know there can be the perception that employees working remotely contribute less than those who work in-person, which isn't true. We wanted to level the playing field to mitigate that kind of bias. So, we were careful to emphasize that managers are to assess employee performance and contributions based on results and metrics, rather than work location."

The extensive work of the cross-organizational team positioned the college to weave a flexible workplace culture into the fabric of the university. "It's a continual process," says the CHRO. "Like any workplace change, the work is never quite done. We continue to keep our pulse on it and infuse it deeper and deeper into our culture."

A flexible work culture starts at the top but must not be created in isolation. Instead, companies are encouraged to take a collaborative approach that welcomes input and ideas from all levels of staff. The COVID-19 pandemic illuminated that a flexible work environment that includes in-person and remote work options can be effective. And research shows that employees want a flexible work culture. To adapt to the changing ways work can be accomplished and meet the interests of employees, companies are encouraged to thoughtfully and collaboratively shift their culture in that direction. This means taking into account ways to equal the playing field so flexible work isn't seen as a women's issue. Companies would do well to frame it as responding to an organizational need that benefits everyone. It also means assessing performance, stretch assignments, sponsorships, and leadership development opportunities based on objective metrics and not to what degree an employee works in the office. This is another way to address the broken-rung phenomenon women leaders face.

Offer Equal Pay

According to Pew Research Center, "The gender gap in pay has remained relatively stable in the United States over the past 15 years or so. In 2020, women earned 84 percent of what men earned, according to. . . analysis of medium hourly earnings of both full- and part-time workers." Pew points out that women would have to work an additional forty-two days in 2020 to earn what men did. The wage gap widens significantly for women of color. A Center for American Progress article points out the following dismal 2020 statistics: Hispanic women earn only 57 cents for every dollar earned by a white, non-Hispanic man, and Black women earn just 64 cents. The economic impact of these inequities is enormous. This amounts to an estimated incredible loss of $1,163,920 for Hispanic women over a forty-year career and $986,240 for Black women.

The gap persists, Pew offers, because of a number of factors, including education level, occupational segregation, gender discrimination, parental leave, career interruptions due to motherhood, and work experience. Additionally, while women keep rising through the ranks, on the whole, they continue to be overrepresented in lower-paying occupations in relation to their share of the workforce, which also contributes to the gender pay gap.

A beacon of light came in May 2022, when the US Soccer Federation announced it reached a collective bargaining agreement to pay the men's and women's national teams equally. The agreement came after a long and arduous battle. It began with a 2016 wage discrimination claim made by five female players to the Equal Opportunity Employment Commission, followed by a class action lawsuit from a group of twenty-eight female players. The legal dispute garnered a good deal of media attention, no doubt boosted by the women's team impressive World Cup championship wins (1991, 1999, 2015, and 2019). The agreement runs through 2028 and includes the equalization of World Cup prize money, identical per-game bonuses, and $22 million in back pay to the women's team. The women's and men's teams will pool their prize money from their respective World Cup appearances and split it equally among them and the federation. As reported by NPR, this makes it the first federation in the world to equalize World Cup prize money. The agreement goes beyond pay. It requires the federation to provide an equal number of charter flights to both the women's and men's teams, as well as equal quality of venues and playing field surfaces. In a statement, US Soccer President Cindy Parlow Cone says, "This is a truly historic moment. These agreements have changed the game forever here in the United States and have the potential to change the game around the world."

Pay inequity affects all aspects of society, including families, mental and physical health, consumer spending, and education attainment. As LeanIn.Org describes, "Closing the pay gap isn't just a win for women—it has social and economic benefits, too. If women were paid fairly, we could cut the poverty rate in half and inject over $500 billion into the US economy." With women making up approximately 54 percent of the workforce in 2022, it's imperative that companies seriously address the issue of equal pay. As described in a 2021 article by the Center for American Progress, women repeatedly identify equal pay and the gender wage gap as top concerns.

Addressing inequities is something that is beneficial to employees and employers alike. "By ensuring employees are paid equitably, employers can increase efficiency, creativity and productivity by helping to attract the best employees, reduce turnover and increase commitment to the organization," Cheryl Pinarchick, an attorney with Fisher Phillips in Boston, says in a 2020 Society for Human Resources Management article.

It's imperative that companies take tangible and sustained action to address equal pay. Companies can review and confront the issue in a number of ways. One is through a pay equity audit. This is a valuable tool used to illuminate information that identifies pay disparities by gathering and analyzing data. Relying on objective data helps crystalize if a company's practices and policies, which may seem neutral on the surface, contribute to pay inequities. A pay equity audit involves comparing the pay of employees performing "like-for-like" work, while taking into consideration reasonable differences such as work experience, credentials, and job performance. The audit also includes examining the causes of pay differences that can't be reasonably explained. Another aspect of the audit is to identify and correct operational gaps that led to the pay discrepancy in the first place. Examples of this include a job being misclassified or decentralized hiring practices where pay is inconsistently applied to the same job. The results of an audit can serve as the starting point for sound policies and practices that then put equal pay into motion.

Committing to publicizing a gender pay analysis is a bold and important step companies can take. In a 2022 post, JUST Capital, an independent nonprofit research organization, reviewed how many of America's largest companies publicly disclose they conduct a gender pay analysis. "This year, we found that just under a quarter of the 954 companies we evaluated in our 2022 Rankings, 23 percent (215 companies), disclose conducting a gender pay gap analysis." Among the 954 companies, only 75 report the exact pay ratios between women and men. Of these 75 companies, a large majority of them have achieved full or near-full pay parity between men and women. Within that group, 28 companies publicly disclose achieving full parity. "These figures tell us that companies continue to release information about their gender pay equity performance only when they are doing well or have achieved their parity goals," notes JUST Capital.

Equileap, an independent data provider of gender metrics, developed a holistic gender equality scorecard that includes nineteen criteria against which they measure companies. Equileap also researches four levels of gender balance: board of directors, executives, senior managers, and workforce. Equileap's 2020 *Gender Equality in the U.S.* report reveals of S&P 500 companies that

- 9 percent have achieved gender balance at the board level;
- 8 percent have achieved gender balance at the executive level;
- 10 percent have achieved gender balance at the management level;
- and 25 percent have a gender-balanced workforce.

Real change can occur only when organizations embrace the importance of pay equity and take active measures to address it. The equal pay gap is real and can't be fixed unless companies take action.

As a leader, you can do your part by asking yourself some questions: What actions can be taken to create pay equity? What compensation and promotion decisions can help everyone succeed more evenly? What policies or practices currently hinder pay equity? What recommendations can be made to the leaders or decision makers above me to address pay inequity?

Corporate Role Models

There are companies that are committed to equal pay as well as gender diversity. By taking a long-term, comprehensive approach, these companies have seen real changes. General Motors is a company that other organizations can look to as a role model. As the only S&P 500 company that doesn't have a gender pay gap, Equileap's 2020 report commends GM on its commitment to fair compensation, publishing their gender gap, making public their strategy to close the gender pay gap, and offering flexible work hours and location. The company also received high marks across Equileap's nineteen criteria, including gender balance at the workforce level, paternal leave, and nondiscriminatory hiring practices.

GM's path to closing the pay gap started long ago and includes many facets. In 2001, it became the first auto company to offer a women's dealer program. Today, their Women's Retail Network (WRN) includes all female dealers and department managers. WRN is committed to filling the pipeline and providing a path forward for women interested in technical and nontechnical careers in the automotive retail sector. This is reflected in their vision: "Our vision is to be an industry leader, with a dealership population that mirrors our communities, by increasing the number of women as dealers, managers, and employees within GM dealerships." At the executive level, in

2014, GM became the first US automobile manufacturer to have a female CEO when Mary Barra was named to the position. Before holding that position, Barra was GM's executive vice president for global product development. Then, in 2018, GM became only the second Fortune 500 company with both a female CEO and CFO when Dhivya Suryadevara was promoted from vice president of corporate finance to CFO. Additionally, GM's board of directors reflects its commitment to diversity. As reported in March 2021 by the *Detroit Free Press*, "Of the women on GM's board one identifies as Hispanic, one as African American, and one as Asian African American, said GM spokesman Jim Cain."

As quoted by the *G20* magazine, Barra said during an interview at Duke University, "To me diversity is all about the pipeline. One of the best kept secrets is that General Motors was working on gender diversity 20 years ago. If I hadn't been pushed and given stretch assignments 20 years ago, I wouldn't have been in a place where I would have been considered for the job I am in now. At GM for all our executive positions we require a diverse slate of candidates, and if they aren't able to have diversity – because they picked this candidate, then we say what are you doing so that in 3 years you will have a diversity of candidates."

L'Oréal is another company highlighted by Equileap. In their *2019 Gender Equality Global Report and Ranking* report, it was the highest ranked French company by Equileap. It discloses pay information by gender, as well as a strategy to address gaps. In addition to paternal leave and flexible work options, L'Oréal publishes all of Equileap's recommended policies to foster gender equality. To help accomplish this, it developed an internal pay measurement tool to monitor equitable pay across its global workforce. It also adopted DE&I policies and practices to ensure equitable career opportunities among its workforce. L'Oréal also enjoys a gender-balanced board and senior management team.

Jean-Claude Le Grand, director of corporate diversity at L'Oréal, is quoted by the *G20 Global Briefing Report* when the company was presented with the Equileap prize for the European-based company with the greatest progress on gender diversity, saying, "We looked around and realised that we had started as a company of men, and we were still a company of men selling products to women! This was not sustainable and we needed to change it. We took the decision but it wasn't something we did overnight, it has taken more than 20 years for us to address every part of this system and to make sure it works, and we are still looking for improvements: can we do this better, would this make a difference. The work never ends." It's apparent that L'Oréal sees gender parity as central to its business and culture. As quoted by *Mirror Review* magazine, Le Grand says, "Even if we are pioneers in gender equality, and if our actions are valued, we must remain committed because we are convinced that gender parity is a performance issue and a key driver for innovation."

A company that has ranked among the top of Equileap's list for several years is Nielsen Holdings, an audience measurement, data, and analytics media company. It has achieved gender balance at the executive, senior management, and workforce levels. Nielsen publishes its gender wage gap and pays employees a living wage. It has set a goal to increase the number of women in senior leadership positions from 39 percent to 46 percent by 2023. In addition, it offers twenty weeks of paid leave for birth mothers and twelve weeks of paid leave for all parents. Nielsen has also established new norms around work flexibility and expanded its mental health and employee assistance programs.

Organizations can look to GM, L'Oréal, and Nielsen as inspirational success stories when it comes to creating a human-centric environment through equal pay and a commitment to gender parity. As these examples illustrate, achieving pay equity takes a concerted effort that must be embedded into the culture and operational aspects of the organization. Conducting a pay equity audit and using Equileap's gender equality scorecard are two tools organizations can leverage in their quest to achieve equal pay status among their workforces. Companies are encouraged to invest the time and resources needed to begin the work today and to sustain it.

Companies that are committed to cultivating a human-centric culture take action to address flexible work and equal pay. Not only do women leaders benefit, but so do the organizations as a whole.

Chapter 10

Women Transforming the World through Fearless Leadership

The undeniable impact of women leaders can be found in the stories of three fearless women: former Prime Minister Jacinda Ardern, Malala Yousafzai, and Alice Paul Tapper. These remarkable individuals relied on their authentic talents and strengths, as well as personal determination, to create tangible, lasting change. I am grateful for the indelible fingerprint they put on society and their commitment to the advancement of women. Their stories illustrate how Collaborative Confidence works in the real world. Their efforts prompted fundamental change that continues to endure and have positive ripple effects for other women. Ardern used her authentic leadership qualities of boldness, decisiveness, and compassion to successfully lead a nation. Malala works tirelessly—risking her own life—to advocate for girls' educational rights. Tapper instills courage, confidence, and character in young girls as they grow into womanhood. Each is a beacon of light that pulls women's leadership forward and changes the world. You too can be a beacon of light that fearlessly illuminates a path forward for the collective good. Practicing

Collaborative Confidence in your workplace, community, and society gives you the path and tools to make transformational change. Each time you highlight the talents and strengths of another woman and encourage her to believe in herself, you create positive change. The same is true when she does this for you. Like Ardern, Malala, and Tapper, you have the capacity to triumphantly move forward, bring other women along with you, and fearlessly generate transformational change.

Female Leadership and Collaboration in Uncertain Times

When the global COVID-19 pandemic hit, we all had to navigate unchartered territory. Significant adjustments were required, whether we were in a leadership position or not. Political leaders, too, had to guide their people through frightening and uncertain times. As the pandemic unfolded, though, it became increasingly clear that countries with the lowest transmission rates had one thing in common: they were led by women. This included then Prime Minister Jacinda Ardern of New Zealand. Her authentic leadership style—which emphasizes trust, accountability, composure, and prioritization of the common good—was well-suited for this crisis. Research backs this up. As described by Jack Zenger and Joseph Folkman in a 2020 *Harvard Business Review* article, women are rated as more effective leaders than men. Their research found this to be true, both before and during the pandemic. "Women were rated more positively on 13 of the 19 competencies that comprise overall leadership effectiveness. Men were rated more positively on one competency—technical/professional expertise—but the difference was not statistically significant." Zenger and Folkman also describe the competencies that direct reports rank as most important during a crisis, which include inspire and motivate, communicate powerfully, collaborate, and build relationships. They add that people also value honest leaders who act with integrity and are sensitive to the stress, anxiety, and frustration of their people. "Our analysis shows that these are the traits that are more often being displayed by women," Zenger and Folkman share in their article.

These are the kinds of qualities Ardern naturally displays. Responding to the COVID-19 pandemic, she embodied a unifying force among New Zealanders by repeatedly referring to them as "our team of five million." In the spirit of Collaborative Confidence, Ardern seemed to know instinctively that navigating the pandemic would require the collective effort of the entire nation.

After officially announcing New Zealand's lockdown, Ardern went on Facebook Live to personally connect with her country's citizens. She continued leveraging the social media platform throughout the height of the pandemic to maintain a personal connection with her people and answer their questions. She provided daily updates clearly explaining the four phases of the country's lockdown plan as well as the conditions that would need to be met to proceed from one phase to the next. Throughout, she balanced the rules and objectives for managing the pandemic while expressing kindness. She ended most of her public appearances with the phrase, "Be strong. Be kind." She remained relatable, sharing her personal struggles during the lockdown, particularly the challenges of being a parent. She also leaned heavily on the scientific experts and stayed in touch with leaders throughout the world. She consistently told New Zealanders the reasons behind her decisions. Her decisive, transparent, and empathetic approach garnered international attention and reminds me of the principles behind executive presence in chapter 5: authentically show up, confidently present yourself, and genuinely connect.

Beginning her political career in 2008 as a member of Parliament, Ardern rose to become New Zealand's prime minister in 2017, when she was only thirty-seven— the world's youngest female leader at the time. Imagine the tightrope she must have walked as her political career transcended, reaching the highest of political offices. She seems to have mastered the balance of being warm and self-assured, caring and tough, and participative and authoritative, which you read about in chapter 6. As described by Carl A. Harte and Supriya Vani in a 2021 *Ms* magazine article, Ardern maintains her authentic personality while "[embodying] astuteness, along with the ability to bring opposing forces together for a greater goal." They describe her as confident and not afraid to share her doubts. "I'm constantly anxious about making mistakes. Everything in politics feels so fragile. I do live in constant fear of what might be," Ardern is quoted as saying in the article. But she doesn't let self-doubt hinder her. It's something she strives to turn into "something more positive," as described in a 2020 interview with the *Guardian*. "I [try to] channel that... 'why am I feeling a bit worried about that, does it mean I need to do a bit more prep, do I need to think more about my decision-making'?"

Another example that illustrates the tightrope Ardern seems to have mastered came less than two months after she became prime minister, when she faced the Christchurch mosque terrorist attacks. She was praised for her compassionate and determined response. Shortly after the attacks, she directly addressed the terrorists. "You may have chosen us, but we utterly reject and condemn you." This was followed by a meeting with Muslim leaders where she asked them what they would like her to do. Wearing a black headscarf as a sign of respect, she hugged many of the victims' families. Later that week, when she addressed the New Zealand Parliament, she opened with the Arabic greeting, *as-salaam alaikum,* which means *peace be with you.* A few days later, Ardern supported sweeping changes to the country's gun laws.

Although her bold response to both the coronavirus pandemic and Christchurch terrorist attacks could have been met with huge resistance, instead it was rewarded with a resounding reelection to office in 2020. As described by Tate Underwood in *Harvard Political Review,* the Labour Party enjoyed many wins in that election. They flipped an additional nineteen seats in Parliament, giving them a solo party majority. The party also gained thirteen percentage points in the party vote, putting the Labour Party above 50 percent in the legislature, which is an incredible feat. "These numbers indicate that New Zealand has rewarded the work of a strong and effective leader who can govern with both strength and empathy." Tate continues,

> Ardern embraces qualities that are both traditionally masculine and feminine, rejecting the premise that leaders must be masculine. Instead of being a stubborn and aggressive leader, Ardern listens to who she represents and communicates her decisions with morals and empathy in mind. At the same time, she is still a leader who is strong enough to take potentially controversial and decisive action. Ardern's active choice to embrace empathy, morality, and openness, traditionally feminine qualities, is what makes her a perfect example of what the leaders of the future should look like.

As Prime Minister, she was also a vocal advocate of gender equality and knows firsthand what it means to be a working mother. In 2018, Ardern became the first head of state to give birth while in office since the late Benazir Bhutto, former prime minister of Pakistan, did so in 1990. Ardern also made headlines as the first world leader to bring her baby to the United Nations General Assembly meeting. In 2020, she made good on the Labour Party's campaign promise to address the gender pay gap by passing the Equal Pay Amendment.

Ardern stands as an inspirational example of what it means to be a leader. She gives us a blueprint that weaves together bold, decisive, and strong qualities with authenticity, compassion, and empathy. These are some of the hallmarks of Collaborative Confidence.

Passionate Advocacy for Girls and Women

Malala Yousafzai is the epitome of a strong, determined, transformational leader who does not allow danger to stand in her way. Even in the face of death threats, she is a steadfast advocate of girls' rights and access to education. Her story is all the more inspiring because her fierce advocacy for girls' education started when she was just a girl herself.

Malala's father was a teacher who ran a girls' school in their Pakistani town. Although raising a girl in Pakistan was not always easy, her father wanted her to have the same opportunities as boys. Malala's passion for learning was apparent from a young age and evidenced by her waddling into her father's classes before she could even talk. She loved school but says, "Everything changed when the Taliban took control of our town in Swat Valley." They banned many aspects of regular life, including school attendance by girls.

With confidence and defiant purpose, Malala spoke out publicly on behalf of girls and their right to learn. At the young age of eleven, she began blogging for the BBC under a pseudonym, Gul Makai. In her blogs, she described the horrors of life under Taliban control. With a strong and steady voice, she became a prominent media guest. In 2011, she was nominated by Archbishop Desmond Tutu for the International Children's Peace Prize. Though her growing platform allowed her to reach more people with her message, it also made her a target. Death threats were published in newspapers, slipped under her door, and posted on Facebook. In October 2012, on her way home from school, a masked gunman boarded the school bus Malala and her friends were riding and shot her in the left side of her head. She was hospitalized and quickly evacuated to a hospital in England where she endured months of surgeries and rehabilitation.

The attempt on her life sparked international media attention, outrage, and support. The Taliban were internationally denounced by governments, human rights organizations, and women's groups. Protests were held in several Pakistani cities the day after the attack, and over two million people signed the Right to Education campaign petition, which led to the ratification of the first Right to Education bill in Pakistan. A United Nations Special Envoy for Global Education launched a petition in Malala's name with three demands:

- We call on Pakistan to agree to plan to deliver education for every child.
- We call on all countries to outlaw discrimination against girls.
- We call on international organizations to ensure the world's sixty-one million out-of-school children are in education by the end of 2015.

The attempt on Malala's life only strengthened her conviction. "It was then I knew I had a choice: I could live a quiet life, or I could make the most of this new life I had been given. I determined to continue my fight until every girl could go to school." In recognition of her work, Malala was awarded the Nobel Peace Prize in 2014 and became the youngest-ever Nobel laureate at age seventeen. Speaking with resolve and confidence at the United Nations in 2013, she said,

> The terrorists thought they would change my aims and stop my ambitions, but nothing changed in my life except this: weakness, fear and hopelessness died. Strength, power and courage was born. . . . I am not against anyone, neither am I here to speak in terms of personal revenge against the Taliban or any other terrorist group. I'm here to speak up for the right of education for every child. I want education for the sons and daughters of the Taliban and all terrorists and extremists.

Malala's relentless dedication to girls' education remains steadfast even now. Throughout all of her dangerous and tumultuous experiences, she has remained connected to her values, inner champion, and strengths. Even as a young activist, her executive presence shone through brightly and remains radiant today. Threats and physical injuries have not deterred her from her purpose and deeply held beliefs. Today, Malala continues to travel to many countries, where she meets with girls fighting poverty, war, child marriage, lack of access to education, and gender discrimination. In 2013, she cofounded the Malala Fund in Birmingham, England, "to champion every girl's right to 12 years of free, safe, quality education." Her 2013 book, *I am Malala: The*

Girl Who Stood Up for Education and Was Shot by the Taliban, became an international bestseller.

Her relentless, authentic, passionate advocacy for girls serves as a beacon of light for the advancement of girls and women everywhere. Her story is a testament to the impact a single woman—young or old—can make, especially when supported by other women. Hers is not a story of singularity, but of plurality. She shows how a single spark can ignite collective change.

Patching Up a Confidence Issue with Innovative Solutions

Alice Paul Tapper is an inspirational and remarkable young woman who epitomizes the meaning of Collaborative Confidence. In 2017, as a young Girl Scout, Tapper made a stark observation that she describes in a *New York Times* op-ed: "On a fourth-grade field trip, I noticed that all the boys stood in the front and raised their hands while most of the girls politely stayed in the back and were quiet. It made me upset." Later, she told her mom, "I thought girls weren't raising their hands because they were afraid that the answer was going to be wrong and that they would be embarrassed. I also think they were being quiet because the boys already had the teacher's attention, and they worried they might not be able to get it." Determined and curious, Tapper talked with the girls in her troop, who agreed it was a problem. Armed with enthusiasm and purpose, Tapper met with Lidia Soto-Harmon, Girl Scouts Nation's Capital CEO (her local council) which represents about fifty thousand girls in the greater Washington DC area. She talked with Soto-Harmon about her idea of a new Girl Scout patch to encourage girls to raise their hands in class and be more confident about speaking up. "We decided to call it the Raise Your Hand patch," Tapper explains. "Its message is that girls should have confidence, step up and become leaders by raising our hands." Just like any other patch, this one must be earned. A Girl Scout has to pledge she'll raise her hand in class and recruit at least three other girls who promise to do the same.

The patch was a hit, garnering widespread attention. Soto-Harmon says in a March 2019 YouTube video, "Across and around the world we started getting emails and calls from folks wanting to get the Raise Your Hand patch. They wanted it for their daughters, their Girl Scout troops, students and even grown women." Soto-Harmon goes on to confirm that young girls struggle with confidence, sharing that according to *The Confidence Code for Girls*, confidence drops 30 percent more for girls than for boys between the ages of eight and fourteen. She adds that this lack of self-assurance can last into adulthood. "At Girl Scouts we recognize that confidence is essential for success. We need to teach girls that failure is okay, risks are worth it, to get out of their comfort zone and raise [their] hand." She tells me the deeper meaning of the patch encourages girls to raise their voice and advocate for things that are important.

The public enthusiasm for the patch garnered attention from some of the largest media outlets. Tapper was interviewed by *Today*, the *Ellen DeGeneres Show*, and CNN, among others. She was also approached by Penguin Young Readers to write a children's book about her experience and the invention of the patch. In it, she tells her own story about feeling embarrassed when she got an answer wrong in class but now having the courage to raise her hand. She also writes about being scared during her first television interview. "I guess that's part of what made me brave. I was afraid, but I did it anyway."

Tapper wants all girls to feel confident and comfortable speaking up: "People say girls have to be 90 percent confident before we raise our hands, but boys just raise their hands. I tell girls we should take the risk and try anyway, just like the boys do. If the answer is wrong, it's not going to end the world. It's not like answering a trivia question wrong to win a million dollars on live TV." Tapper continues to pay it forward by donating the proceeds from her book to support the Girl Scouts.

Alice Paul Tapper's story of the Raise Your Hand patch is a source of inspiration that beautifully weaves together many of the threads of Collaborative Confidence. Earning the patch by raising your hand and encouraging other girls to do the same is a perfect demonstration of the reciprocal nature of Collaborative Confidence. It also threads in the practice of amplification, allowing you to showcase your leadership and spotlight the contributions of other women. Alice Paul Tapper brought forth her inner champion and helped other girls do the same. Now, it's your turn to practice Collaborative Confidence. Raise your hand and encourage other women around you to do the same.

Final Thoughts

The Promise of Collaborative Confidence

When you engage in Collaborative Confidence, you make this simple promise to yourself and others: "I am responsible for my own confidence and for helping other women with theirs." Collaborative Confidence is reciprocal and relational, and when practiced daily with authenticity and consistency, it has the power to magnify qualities women are often known for—compassion, empathy, and courage. When women discover and tap into their own unique talents and powers as well as those of other women, it awakens an unstoppable transformational force.

Recall the stories shared in *Collaborative Confidence*—the women in the Obama administration, who amplified each other's ideas; Angie Hicks, who successfully navigated the tightrope of self-promotion; Shalane Flanagan, who created a world-renowned running club for female distance runners; Condoleezza Rice, who established herself as an expert, which garnered her national and international prominence; Jacinda Ardern, who led her nation with her compassionate and empathetic heart as well as bold, decisive thinking; Malala, who relentlessly advocates for the advancement of girls, even at the risk of her own life; and Alice Paul Tapper, who created a Girl Scout patch that gained national attention and encourages girls to speak up. Also, remember the many less well-known women leaders whose stories also demonstrated Collaborative Confidence at work. Let their stories inspire, guide, and encourage you to take purposeful action on behalf of yourself and other women. When women activate their self-awareness and amplify each other, transformational change for everyone becomes possible. And when organizations take bold action to accelerate transformational change, then environments in which women leaders can truly thrive are created. Research shows us that organizations can benefit when human-centric corporate cultures are nurtured.

You are a strong, capable, talented woman leader. Collaborative Confidence is your opportunity to cultivate the remarkable woman you are and encourage other women to do the same. As you weave Collaborative Confidence into your everyday life, you create enduring bonds with other women. This will propel you *all* forward. Each of you will become a source of inspiration to other women—showing them the extraordinary power and nurturing support that comes from Collaborative Confidence. In turn, this creates a ripple effect that can reach further than any of you could as individuals. Seize today. Create an enduring bond with at least one other woman and set in motion this powerful ripple effect.

Remember and practice the strategies you learned in the pages of this book. Activate your self-awareness. Amplify your ideas as well as those of other women. Encourage your employer to accelerate workplace change. Resolve to start practicing Collaborative Confidence today and watch its promise unfold all around you.

Resources

Through joining together, we can change the face of leadership and transform the world of work. Countless organizations are on that very quest. Their dedicated efforts make a difference and create environments that foster strong female leadership. Organizations including Chief, LeanIn.Org, the Women's Impact Alliance, and Women Together advocate for the advancement of women leaders. Nonprofits such as Girls Who Code work to close the gender gap in computer technology. These organizations, as well as others like them, are the beacons of gravitational light that pull women's leadership forward.

Chief

Chief is an organization that is committed to propelling women into leadership positions and keeping them there. Founded in 2019 by Lindsay Kaplan and Carolyn Childers, Chief is a private network for women in powerful leadership positions, from rising vice president level to CEO, as well as company founders. Chief is dedicated to strengthening women's leadership, magnifying women's influence, and paving the way so other women are brought along with them.

As described by Childers during a podcast interview with *Inc. Founders Project with Alexa von Tobel*, she and Kaplan relied on their own professional experiences as the beginning point of what would become Chief: "We were both more senior women executives in the start-up worlds and we're just starting to realize how much time we were spending mentoring other people, managing our teams and actually felt like we had no real investment into ourselves as leaders and no community for us to go to build that." She goes on to explain how that was coupled with a societal shift that put an emphasis on the importance of women's leadership: "[We] said there needs to be something for a senior woman executive and the idea of building a community that drives more women into the C-suite and supports them when they get there is just so important."

Kaplan relays her own experience in a 2021 interview with *Jewish Insider,* when she was promoted to a vice president position: "I needed more support, more guidance, more mentorship than ever. And yet that's also the moment when I became the de facto mentor for women in my organization." She goes on to add, "Because if it's lonely at the top, it gets lonely a lot faster when you're a woman." Anne, a Chief member, talks of her experience, saying, "The biggest benefit I get from Chief is the peer network of other women leaders. As you move into senior leadership roles you can't share your ups and downs with too many people, and there's more added pressure to get things done and be successful. Having a peer network of women leaders who are going through similar things gives me more confidence because it validates what I'm experiencing. Because of Chief and the remarkable women I've met there, I know I'm not the only one dealing with the stresses and hard things about being an executive woman leader. The feeling of support is unbelievable."

The dismally small number of women in executive leadership positions also motivated Kaplan and Childers to found Chief. As put by Kaplan during the *Inc. Founders* podcast, "You see conversations about women in the workplace now more than ever and yet those numbers haven't moved at all. So, we really wanted to make a difference and we really wanted to do it as quickly as possible because we don't have the patience to wait decades, to wait generations, to see equality in the C-suite." Complementing this sentiment, Nicole, a Chief member, says, "As women leaders we learn from each other, get different points of view, and soak up inspiration and practical strategies that help move us up and forward."

Described as a "private network for the most powerful women in leadership," Chief connects high-level women leaders with each other to support and accelerate their professional trajectory. A centerpiece of their offerings is a peer advisory group referred to as a core group. Core groups are a curated cohort that meet monthly and are facilitated by an executive coach. I'm fortunate to be one of their coaches and have experienced firsthand the transformation women experience from being in a group of peers where they can talk openly and honestly. Nicole says of her experience, "There's such a strong connection in my core group. It's reassuring to know that so many other accomplished women also struggle with insecurities, decision-making, and wondering if they're leading their teams the best they can. I don't have all the answers and in my core group we talk in a way that's open and vulnerable. And we bounce around strategies that can be used in different situations. That kind of support and authenticity makes it a rich experience." Anne shares her core group experience, saying, "It's given me more confidence as a leader because it validates my experiences and feelings and gives me ways to solve problems. Having real conversations with real women in similar positions means I'm not on an island dealing with things in isolation."

Chief also offers a myriad of cutting-edge leadership resources, including content about equal pay, negotiating, global economics, and diversity, equity, and inclusion. Known for their guest speakers, Chief brings in powerhouses such as media mogul Shonda Rhimes, Bonobos cofounder and former CEO Andy Dunn, former first lady Michelle Obama, and Yale University professor Dr. Laurie Santos.

Anne and Nicole speak of the spirit of Collaborative Confidence they find at Chief. "Chief shows me how valuable a network of women in a similar phase of their career is," says Nicole. "You leave every conversation feeling good about what you learned and the help you've given another woman." Anne concurs, adding, "The whole ethos of women coming together to share their triumphs and struggles aligns perfectly with Collaborative Confidence. Being a Chief member means I get to help other women and they get to help me."

Website: chief.com
Email: hello@chief.com

LeanIn.Org

LeanIn.Org knows that leaning in isn't a solo act. The leaders of this organization understand that the support of a community of women—where common struggles can be shared, challenges tackled, and successes celebrated—is a powerful force. LeanIn.Org supports women through community engagement, educational opportunities, research, and peer groups referred to as circles. The springboard of the organization came following the 2013 release of Sheryl Sandberg's bestselling book, *Lean In: Women, Work, and the Will to Lead*. Today, with its mission to "help women achieve their ambitions and work to create an equal world," there are more than 35,000 LeanIn.Org circles with over 380,000 members in more than 150 countries.

Centered on the belief that "there's power in women coming together," circles provide a rich network of peer support and facilitated discussions. As quoted in a 2018 *New York Times* article, Rachel Thomas, president of LeanIn.Org says, "Circles are one of the few places in the world where women can be overtly, unapologetically ambitious." Interviewed by the *New York Times,* nuclear engineer and commanding officer Emily Bassett says of her experience as a LeanIn circle member, "I attribute much of my confidence to what I learned there." She adds, "One thing LeanIn made me realize is that you are never alone with your leadership issues. We can get lost in our own headspace sometimes. But you learn that there is always someone else having the same issue." In addition to her circle experience, Bassett found through LeanIn.Org a treasure trove of resources on a myriad of leadership topics, including giving feedback, negotiating, managing your body language, and more. Inspired by her experience, she cofounded four circles especially for military personnel, two of which are coed.

In addition to the peer-based circles, LeanIn.Org is a fierce advocate committed to "[advocating] for better public policies and a more equitable workplace because to make lasting change, we need institutional change." The organization wants to see women not only succeed but excel, including breaking down barriers that hold them back. "We want all women to be paid fairly, treated with respect, and given equal opportunities to learn, grow, and lead. We want to kick bias out of the workplaces and everywhere, because no one should be treated unfairly because of who they are—and because inclusive workplaces bring out the best in everyone. Together, we can make work work for women in a way it never has before."

Like Collaborative Confidence, LeanIn.Org knows that together women are more powerful than they are alone and that support comes from having a committed community in your corner—a community that cheers you on when you're down, washes away your fears when you doubt yourself, encourages you to take risks, and celebrates your successes with every forward step you take. "Anything is possible when women come together to share their experiences, build new skills, and cheer each other on."

Website: leanin.org
Email: info@leanin.org

The Women's Impact Alliance

An organization dedicated to cultivating the talents and skills of young female leaders, the Women's Impact Alliance (WIA), previously known as the Coaching Fellowship, was founded by Jane Finette in 2014. WIA provides leadership programs for early career women who have dedicated their professional lives to social and environmental change. Its humble beginnings stem back to Finette graciously offering three pro bono coaching sessions to young women professionals. Her heartfelt generosity was rooted in the desire to give back her own time to a handful of women who were beginning their professional journey. Today, that seed of generosity has grown into an organization that serves more than 200 young women annually through yearlong leadership development programs. More than 1,500 women representing over 80 countries have now been through these programs. WIA serves these young leaders with their more than 220 volunteer coaches from over 32 countries. I am proud to be among that cadre of coach volunteers and support the incredible mission of WIA. With Finette's passionate advocacy and steadfast drive for young women, it's no surprise how the organization's reach has grown.

The women leader participants are dedicated to building a more sustainable future for the world. Finette is passionate about "equipping these young leaders as they progress in their careers. The global grand challenges they are undertaking and the problems of our planet are becoming too numerous to solve. We want to accelerate the change they are making by giving them an opportunity to grow their leadership capacity."

She recalls one story in particular about a program participant from Uganda. The participant was thriving at the organization in which she worked and then was unexpectedly asked to temporarily step into the role of executive director. Later, she told Jane that had she not been in WIA's program and had the support of a coach and network of peers, she would not have accepted the role. Today, she is officially the executive director and has doubled the size of the organization. Finette offers, "We don't know when an opportunity may come our way and if you don't have someone in your corner—a group of strong allies—when that something comes knocking you might not accept it. For her, she had someone in her corner. It's so vitally important."

The backbone behind Finette's steadfast dedication to support early career women leaders is articulated in the organization's mission: "We believe that through a combination of leadership development, coaching, and community at a crucial point in their career, women leaders will manifest the change they want to be and see in the world faster and at an exponentially greater scale."

WIA's carefully curated approach includes one-on-one coaching, peer forums, and leader-lab practice modules. This combination aims to increase the leadership capacity of the participants, including boosting their confidence and courage, building their strengths, and aligning their values with action.

Finette is a fierce advocate of women supporting women and the immense power that comes from it. As she says, "Every woman can help every sister rise and thrive." She also knows that this can't be done alone or in a vacuum. She goes on to say, "In order to make significant and lasting change happen we need new legislation, people, business, governments to be held accountable and we need to work together to make gender and racial bias a thing of the past."

It's Finette's steadfast belief of "when we lift another woman, we all rise" that undergirds her work and the work of WIA. It also aligns with the meaning and power of Collaborative Confidence. The immeasurable power of the collective cannot be undersold. It is a powerful force that creates transformation.

Website: www.thewia.org
Email: hello@thewia.org

Women Together

Founded in 2019 by clothing designer Eileen Fisher, Women Together is a place where women can find comfort and confidence, just as Fisher wants women to feel in the clothes she creates. Women Together's mission is to "support and inspire you as you build a more mindful, embodied life—a life that's infused with purpose and meaning."

There are a myriad of resources and ways to engage in all that Women Together has to offer, including workshops, events, videos, articles, exercises, and guidebooks. "Through sharing, generous listening, movement, and reflection our on-line and in-person experiences empower us to activate our inner strength." Women Together offers small groups, called Conversations, that provide a sanctuary for meaningful conversations, deep connections, and exchange of personal insights. Another offering, Life Notes, is a library of articles and videos where you can soak up inspiration and wisdom anytime you want. Life Notes covers a broad range of topics, including self-love, resilience, leading like a woman, negotiating a raise, emotional triggers, compassion, mindfulness, and decision-making. Another program is an interactive live-stream called CONNECT that allows women to share their voices, draw on their strengths, and uplift and encourage one another. CONNECT is a place to explore topics, share experiences, and discover tools.

Connecting women is at the heart of what Women Together does. "I believe that a powerful collective energy emerges when women connect with other women," says Fisher.

Website: womentogether.com
Email: Use website contact form

Girls Who Code

The gender gap isn't confined to pay or title. It can be found in industries as well. Girls Who Code is a remarkable nonprofit organization that "is on a mission to close the gender gap in technology and to change the image of what a programmer looks like and does." To do this, they offer student clubs, summer programs, and college and career services. Girls Who Code is changing the face of technology through legislation, as well as by working with policy makers "to close the gender gap in K-12 computer science classrooms."

The economics are clear. Their 2019 *Advocacy Report: The state of girls in K-12 classrooms* reveals, "Computing jobs are among the fastest growing in the U.S. economy. These jobs pay more than double the average U.S. salary. And in the coming years will be key drivers of national economic growth and mobility." The report says the participation rate in computer science courses among K-12 girls overall is 37.5 percent, while it's only 15.5 percent for historically underrepresented girls. With fierce determination, they are on a mission to increase that.

Girls Who Code was founded in 2012 by Reshma Saujani. She noticed how few girls were in computer science classes and took action to change that. Another problem she wanted to address is that, as she argues, girls are raised to be perfect, while boys are raised to be brave. With Girls Who Code, she socializes young girls to be brave by taking risks and learning to do computer programming. When girls enter the program, their fear is apparent. In a 2016 TED talk Saujani says, "We immediately see in our program our girls' fear of not getting it right, not being perfect." She goes on to say, "What I found is that by teaching them to code I had socialized them to be brave." The similarities Saujani sees between young girls and women is striking: "I can't tell you how many women tell me 'I'm afraid to raise my hand. I'm afraid to ask a question because I don't want to be the only one who doesn't understand. The only one who is struggling.' When we teach girls to be brave and we have a supportive networking cheering them they will build incredible things."

Increasing the number and visibility of women in technology through their programs for young girls is at the heart of what Girls Who Code does. To that end, they offer free lesson plans that feature women pioneers in tech, both historical and modern-day. The aim is to help girls see themselves in these pioneers and cause them to think differently about who can be successful in coding. A celebratory milestone came in 2021, when more than 80,000 Girls Who Code alumnae entered the workforce. As of March 2021, their programs have reached more than 300,000 girls globally.

The road ahead may not be easy, but the reward is incredible. As the organization's 2019 report says, "At Girls Who Code, we believe that closing the gender gap will take rooting out bias and discrimination still widespread at every stage in the pipeline. It will take building girls' bravery and resilience, making them feel like they belong, and demonstrating that they can use tech to solve problems they care about. At the center of this work is the need for thoughtful policies that take gender into account. The support of national, state, and local governments are crucial parts of our efforts to making our classrooms more diverse."

As Saujani says in her TED talk, "We cannot wait for [girls] to learn to be brave. We have to teach them in schools and early in their careers when it has the most potential to impact their lives, and the lives of others. And we have to show them that they will be loved and accepted not for being perfect but for being courageous." Uplifting girls so they know they are brave, courageous, and incredibly capable is the seed that continues to grow and blossom as girls move into womanhood.

Website: girlswhocode.com
Email: info@girlswhocode.com

References

INTRODUCTION

Eilperin, J. (2021, October 28). *White House women want to be in the room where it happens.* The Washington Post. Retrieved June 6, 2021, from https://www.washingtonpost.com/news/powerpost/wp/2016/09/13/white-house-women-are-now-in-the-room-where-it-happens/

The qualities that distinguish women leaders. Caliper. (n.d.). Retrieved June 21, 2021, from https://www.calipercanada.com/portfolio/the-qualities-that-distinguish-women-leaders/

CHAPTER 1

Tasha Eurich. (2018, January 4). *What self-awareness really is (and how to cultivate it).* Harvard Business Review. Retrieved July 8, 2021, from https://hbr.org/2018/01/what-self-awareness-really-is-and-how-to-cultivate-it

Korn Ferry. (2021, April 15). *A better return on self-awareness.* Korn Ferry. Retrieved July 10, 2021, from https://www.kornferry.com/insights/briefings-magazine/issue-17/better-return-self-awareness

Flaum, J. P. (n.d.). *When it comes to business leadership, Nice Guys Finish first - green peak.* Retrieved July 10, 2021, from https://green-

peakpartners.com/wp-content/uploads/2018/09/Green-Peak_
Cornell-University-Study_What-predicts-success.pdf

Dierdorff, E. C., & Rubin, R. S. (2017, December 6). *Research: We're not very self-aware, especially at work.* Harvard Business Review. Retrieved July 12, 2021, from https://hbr.org/2015/03/researc h-were-not-very-self-aware-especially-at-work

Raghunathan, R. (2013, October 10). *How negative is your "mental chatter"?* Psychology Today. Retrieved July 12, 2021, from https:// www.psychologytoday.com/us/blog/sapient-nature/201310/ho w-negative-is-your-mental-chatter

Gyalwa, T. (n.d.). *Benefits of meditation for the mind and body.* Mindworks Meditation. Retrieved July 2, 2021, from https:// mindworks.org/blog/benefits-meditation-mind-body/

CHAPTER TWO

Chamine, S. (2016). *Positive intelligence: Why only 20% of teams and individuals achieve their true potential And How You can achieve yours.* Greenleaf Book Group Press.

Brain anatomy and how the brain works. Brain Anatomy and How the Brain Works | Johns Hopkins Medicine. (2021, July 14). Retrieved August 3, 2021, from https://www.hopkinsmedicine.org/health/ conditions-and-diseases/anatomy-of-the-brain

Florida International University - Digital Communications, J. Z. (n.d.). *Untangling the tightrope that female leaders need to walk: Groundbreaking work wins 2020 Alvah H. Chapman Jr.. outstanding dissertation award.* FIU. Retrieved August 23, 2021, from https://lead.fiu.edu/resources/news/categories/ untangling-the-tightrope.html

Zheng, W., Kark, R., & Meister, A. (2018, November 28). *How women manage the gendered norms of leadership.* Harvard Business Review. Retrieved August 11, 2021, from https://hbr.org/2018/11/ho w-women-manage-the-gendered-norms-of-leadership

Women are "bossy" and men are "decisive" – ecornell #IMPACT. (2018, January 24). Retrieved August 4, 2021, from https://ecornell-impact. cornell.edu/women-are-bossy-and-men-are-decisive/

Holzel, B. K., Carmody, J., Evans, K. C., Hoge, E. A., Dusek, J. A., Morgan, L., Pitman, R. K., & Lazar, S. W. (2009, September 23.). *Stress reduction correlates with structural changes in the amygdala.* Academic. oup.com. Retrieved August 7, 2021, from https://academic.oup. com/scan/article/5/1/11/1728269?login=true#126919244

Bullock B Grace Bullock B Grace Bullock, B. G. (n.d.). *What focusing on the breath does to your brain.* Greater Good. Retrieved August 8, 2021, from https://greatergood.berkeley.edu/article/item/ what_focusing_on_the_breath_does_to_your_brain

Herrero, J. L., Khuvis, S., Yeagle, E., Cerf, M., & Mehta, A. D. (2018, January 3). *Breathing above the brain stem: Volitional control and attentional modulation in humans.* Journal of Neurophysiology. Retrieved August 7, 2021, from https://journals.physiology.org/ doi/full/10.1152/jn.00551.2017

Keysers, C., & Gazzola, V. (2014, April 28). *Hebbian learning and predictive mirror neurons for actions, sensations and emotions.* Philosophical transactions of the Royal Society of London. Series B, Biological sciences. Retrieved August 11, 2021, from https:// www.ncbi.nlm.nih.gov/pmc/articles/

CHAPTER THREE

Roiz, J. (2021, July 9). *Sarah Duru celebrates French Toast Agency's 10th anniversary: 'I had to make a name for myself'*. Billboard. Retrieved August 14, 2021, from https://www.billboard.com/music/latin/french-toast-agency-anniversary-interview-9598986/

Lencioni, P. M. (2022, September 13). *Make your values mean something*. Harvard Business Review. Retrieved August 14, 2021, from https://hbr.org/2002/07/make-your-values-mean-something

Importance of defining a company's core values. Business Class: Trends and Insights | American Express. (n.d.). Retrieved August 15, 2021, from https://www.americanexpress.com/en-ca/business/trends-and-insights/articles/importance-of-defining-a-companys-core-values/

Dvorak, N., & Schatz, J. (2020, May 11). *A guiding star during coronavirus: Your company values*. Gallup.com. Retrieved August 15, 2021, from https://www.gallup.com/workplace/310430/guiding-star-during-coronavirus-company-values.aspx

Chowdhury, M. R. (2019, August 12). *The 3 best questionnaires for Measuring Values*. PositivePsychology.com. Retrieved August 19, 2021, from https://positivepsychology.com/values-questionnaire/

George, B. (2015). *Discover your true north*. John Wiley & Sons, Inc.

Schneider, K.J., Bugental, J. and Pierson, F.J. (2001) *Handbook of Humanistic Psychology*. Thousand Oaks, CA: Sage.

CHAPTER FOUR

Gallup, I. (2022, October 11). *Science of Clifton Strengths*. Gallup.com. Retrieved September 15, 2021, from https://www.gallup.com/cliftonstrengths/en/253790/science-of-cliftonstrengths.aspx

Harter, J. (2020, July 2). *Historic drop in employee engagement follows record rise.* Gallup.com. Retrieved September 9, 2021, from https://www.gallup.com/workplace/313313/historic-drop-employee-engagement-follows-record-rise.aspx

Rigoni, B., & Asplund, J. (2022, November 16). *Strengths-based employee development: The business results.* Gallup.com. Retrieved September 16, 2021, from https://www.gallup.com/workplace/236297/strengths-based-employee-development-business-results.aspx

Harter, J., & Adkins, A. (2021, August 30). *What great managers do to engage employees.* Harvard Business Review. Retrieved October 2, 2021, from https://hbr.org/2015/04/what-great-managers-do-to-engage- employees

Buckingham, M., & Clifton, D. O. (2005). *Now, discover your strengths.* Pocket Books.

Defining strengths. Marcus Buckingham. (2020, September 2). Retrieved September 17, 2021, from https://www.marcusbuckingham.com/defining-strengths/

Invest in your strengths. Marcus Buckingham. (2020, September 2). Retrieved September 17, 2021, from https://www.marcusbuckingham.com/invest-in-your-strengths-2/

Freij, A. (2017, April 10). *Strengths and positive psychology: The strengths recipe for Success.* PositivePsychology.org.uk. Retrieved September 17, 2021, from http://positivepsychology.org.uk/strengths-recipe-for-success

Ackerman, C. E. (2019, May 6). *Understanding leadership strengths in the workplace.* PositivePsychology.com. Retrieved September 8, 2021, from https://positivepsychology.com/leadership-strengths/

Sorenson, S. (n.d.). *How employees' strengths make your company stronger.* Gallup.com. Retrieved September 30, 2021, from https://

www.gallup.com/workplace/231605/employees-strengths-company-stronger.aspx

You searched for strengths. PositivePsychology.com. (n.d.). Retrieved September 30, 2021, from https://positivepsychology.com/?s=strengths

Marcus, B. (2005). *What great managers do.* Harvard Business Review. Retrieved October 1, 2021, from https://hbr.org/2005/03/what-great-managers-do

Jones, D. J. and, & Buono, J. (2019, May 3). *To unleash people's strengths, help them manage weaknesses.* Gallup.com. Retrieved October 2, 2021, from https://www.gallup.com/cliftonstrengths/en/266435/unleash-people-strengths-help-manage-weaknesses.aspx

Flade, P., Asplund, J., & Elliot, G. (2015, October 8). *Employees who use their strengths outperform those who don't.* Gallup.com. Retrieved October 5, 2021, from https://www.gallup.com/workplace/236561/employees-strengths-outperform-don.aspx

CHAPTER FIVE

Hinchliffe, E. (2021, June 2). *The female CEOS on this year's Fortune 500 just broke three all-time records.* Fortune. Retrieved December 9, 2022, from https://fortune.com/2021/06/02/female-ceos-fortune-500-2021-women-ceo-list-roz-brewer-walgreens-karen-lynch-cvs-thasunda-brown-duckett-tiaa/

Mayo, M. (2016, July 8). *To seem confident, women have to be seen as warm.* Harvard Business Review. Retrieved December 9, 2022, from https://hbr.org/2016/07/to-seem-confident-women-have-to-be-seen-as-warm

Khan, S. (2020, February 13). *Council post: Hack your executive presence: Five research-backed tips to instant gravitas.* Forbes. Retrieved

December 1, 2022, from https://www.forbes.com/sites/forbes-coachescouncil/2020/02/13/hack-your-executive-presence-five-research-backed-tips-to-instant-gravitas/?sh=72ee444372da

Newton, R. (2020, September 24). *Gravitas is a quality you can develop.* Harvard Business Review. Retrieved December 3, 2022, from https://hbr.org/2020/09/gravitas-is-a-quality-you-can-develop

Smith, D. D. (2021, June 30). *If you want to lead, master this skill.* Harvard Business Review. Retrieved December 3, 2021, from https://hbr.org/2021/06/if-you-want-to-lead-master-this-skill

Zandan, N. (2018, August 1). *How to stop saying "um," "ah," and "you know".* Harvard Business Review. Retrieved November 30, 2021, from https://hbr.org/2018/08/how-to-stop-saying-um-ah-and-you-know

Daimler, M. (2016, May 25). *Listening is an overlooked leadership tool.* Harvard Business Review. Retrieved November 29, 2021, from https://hbr.org/2016/05/listening-is-an-overlooked-leadership-tool

Chng, D. H. M., Kim, T.-Y., Gilbreath, B., & Andersson, L. (2018, August 17). *Why people believe in their leaders - or not.* MIT Sloan Management Review. Retrieved December 13, 2021, from https://sloanreview.mit.edu/article/why-people-believe-in-their-leaders-or-not/

Riggio, R. E. (2021, September 10). *How to increase your leadership credibility.* Psychology Today. Retrieved December 17, 2021, from https://www.psychologytoday.com/us/blog/cutting-edge-leadershiphow-increase-your-leadership-credibility

How leaders build trust. Harvard Business Review. (2019, June 26). Retrieved December 1, 2021, from https://hbr.org/tip/2019/06/how-leaders-build-trust

Ouslis, N. (2019, February 11). *Trust in leadership - one key factor during Organizational Change • Scienceforwork*. ScienceForWork. Retrieved December 11, 2021, from https://scienceforwork.com/blog/trust-in-leadership-change/

Nelson, B. (2021, December 9). *Great leaders have these behaviors in common*. Gallup.com. Retrieved December 22, 2021, from https://www.gallup.com/cliftonstrengths/en/357983/great-leaders-behaviors-common.aspx

Camarote, R. (n.d.). *The best leaders know these 6 tricks to being more approachable*. Retrieved December 11, 2021, from https://www.inc.com/robin-camarote/the-best-leaders-know-these-6-tricks-to-being-more-approachable.html

Van Bommel, T. (2022) *The power of empathy in times of crisis and beyond (report), Catalyst*. Available at: https://www.catalyst.org/reports/empathy-work-strategy-crisis (Accessed: December 8, 2021).

Schneider, M. (n.d.). *A google study revealed that the best managers use emotional ... - inc.com*. Inc. Retrieved December 15, 2021, from https://www.inc.com/michael-schneider/a-google-study-revealed-that-best-managers-use-emotional-intelligence-share-this-1-trait.html

Zaki, J. (2019, May 30). *Making empathy central to your company culture*. Harvard Business Review. Retrieved December 5, 2021, from https://hbr.org/2019/05/making-empathy-central-to-your-company-culture

Bigman, D., & Buss, D. (2021, July 16). *The remarkable power of Gratitude*. ChiefExecutive.net. Retrieved December 8, 2021, from https://chiefexecutive.net/the-remarkable-power-of-gratitude/

Roberts Gibson, K., O'Leary, K., & Weintraub, J. R. (2020, January 24). *The little things that make employees feel appreciated*.

Harvard Business Review. Retrieved December 20, 2021, from https://hbr.org/2020/01/the-little-things-that-mak e-employees-feel-appreciated

Dolan, E. W. (2017, October 30). *Study reveals just how quickly we form a first impression.* PsyPost. Retrieved December 4, 2021, from https://www.psypost.org/2017/10/study-reveals-just-quickly-for m-first-impression-50039

Economy, P. (2018, December 29). *According to this truly surprising new study, you have just 27 seconds ...* Inc.com. Retrieved December 4, 2021, from https://www.inc.com/peter-economy/ according-to-this-truly-surprising-new-study-you-have-j ust-27-seconds-to-make-a-first-impression.html

Okten, I. O. (2018, January 31). *Studying first impressions: What to consider?* Association for Psychological Science - APS. Retrieved December 9, 2021, from https://www.psychologicalscience.org/ observer/studying-first-impressions-what-to-consider

CHAPTER SIX

Exley, C., & Kessler, J. (2019, December 19). *Why don't women self-promote as much as men?* Harvard Business Review. Retrieved February 1, 2022, from https://hbr.org/2019/12/why-don t-women-self-promote-as-much-as-men

Zbar, J. (2020, August 31). *Untangling the tightrope that female leaders need to walk: Groundbreaking work wins 2020 Alvah H. Chapman Jr.. outstanding dissertation award.* Lead.FIU.Edu/Resources. Retrieved February 13, 2022, from https://lead.fiu.edu/re- sources/news/categories/untangling-the-tightrope.html

Thomson, S. (2018, September 20). *A lack of confidence isn't what's hold- ing back working women.* The Atlantic. Retrieved February 4, 2022, from https://www.theatlantic.com/family/archive/2018/09/women-workplace-confidence-gap/570772/

Ro, C. (2021, January 19). *Why do we still distrust women leaders?* BBC Worklife. Retrieved February 23, 2022, from https://www.bbc.com/worklife/article/20210108-why-do-we-still-distrust-women-leaders

Zheng, W., Kark, R., & Meister, A. (2018, November 28). *How women manage the gendered norms of leadership.* Harvard Business Review. Retrieved February 11, 2022, from https://hbr.org/2018/11/how-women-manage-the-gendered-norms-of-leadership

Schwarb, J. (2013, February 19). *Angie Hicks: The woman behind angie's list.* Indianapolis Monthly. Retrieved February 3, 2022, from https://www.indianapolismonthly.com/news-and-opinion/business/angie-hicks-the-woman-behind-angies-list

Profile - entrepreneurship - Harvard Business School. Entrepreneurship. (2000). Retrieved February 3, 2022, from https://entrepreneurship.hbs.edu/founders/Pages/profile.aspx?num=18

The self-promotion gap. The Self-Promotion Gap. (n.d.). Retrieved February 18, 2022, from https://www.selfpromotiongap.com/

Correll, S. J., & Nishiura Mackenzie, L. (2016, September 13). *To succeed in Tech, women need more visibility.* Harvard Business Review. Retrieved February 11, 2022, from https://hbr.org/2016/09/to-succeed-in-tech-women-need-more-visibility

O'Kane, C. (2020) *"Mr. vice president, I'm speaking": Kamala Harris rebukes pence's interruptions during debate, CBS News.* CBS Interactive. Available at: https://www.cbsnews.com/news/kamala-harris-mr-vice-president-pence-interruptions/ (Accessed: February 2, 2022).

Ibarra, H. (2019, September 19). *A lack of sponsorship is keeping women from advancing into leadership.* Harvard Business Review. Retrieved

February 9, 2022, from https://hbr.org/2019/08/a-lack-of-spons orship-is-keeping-women-from-advancing-into-leadership

For the Center for Diversity, inclusion, and belonging's fifth anniversary, justice Sonia Sotomayor discusses the importance of diversity. For the Center for Diversity, Inclusion, and Belonging's fifth anniversary, Justice Sonia Sotomayor discusses the importance of diversity | NYU School of Law. (2021, October 26). Retrieved February 21, 2022, from https://www.law.nyu.edu/news/CDI B-Sonia-Sotomayor-Kenji-Yoshino-five-anniversary

Jacobi, T., & Schweers, D. (2017, April 11). *Female Supreme Court justices are interrupted more by male justices and advocates.* Harvard Business Review. Retrieved February 20, 2022, from https://hbr. org/2017/04/female-supreme-court-justices-are-interrupted-m ore-by-male-justices-and-advocates

Grant, A. (2021, February 18). *Perspective | who won't shut up in meetings? men say it's women. it's not.* The Washington Post. Retrieved February 23, 2022, from https://www.washingtonpost.com/ outlook/2021/02/18/men-interrupt-women-tokyo-olympics/

Pietersen, K. (2015). *KP: The autobiography.* Amazon. Retrieved February 23, 2022, from https://read.amazon.com/kp

CHAPTER SEVEN

Eilperin, J. (2016, September 13). *White House women want to be in the room where it happens.* The Washington Post. Retrieved January 7, 2022, from https://www.washingtonpost.com/news/ powerpost/wp/2016/09/13/white-house-women-are-now-in-th e-room-where-it-happens/

Eilperin, J. (2016, October 25). *How a white house women's office strategy went viral.* The Washington Post. Retrieved January

7, 2022, from https://www.washingtonpost.com/news/pow-erpost/wp/2016/10/25/how-a-white-house-womens-offic e-strategy-went-viral/

Bain, K., Kreps, T. A., Meikle, N. L., & Tenney, E. R. (2021, June 17). *Research: Amplifying your colleagues' voices benefits every-one.* Harvard Business Review. Retrieved April 6, 2022, from https://hbr.org/2021/06/research-amplifying-your-colleague s-voices-benefits-everyone

Rojas, M. (2021, August 3). *Dear female job seeker: Apply for the job, ignore the 'qualifications.'* FastCompany.com. Retrieved April 30, 2022, from https://www.fastcompany.com/90661349/dea r-female-jobseeker-apply-for-the-job-ignore-the-qualifications

Shine theory. Shine Theory. (n.d.). Retrieved February 1, 2022, from https://www.shinetheory.com/

Fostering Women's Leadership & Workplace Inclusion. Lean In. (n.d.). Retrieved April 9, 2022, from https://leanin.org/

Women have always been powerful. Chief. (n.d.). Retrieved April 29, 2022, from https://chief.com/

Home. (n.d.). Women Together. Retrieved April 22, 2022, from https://womentogether.com/

Crouse, L. (2017, November 11). *How the 'shalane flanagan effect' works.* The New York Times. Retrieved May 3, 2022, from https://www.nytimes.com/2017/11/11/opinion/sunday/shalan e-flanagan-marathon-running.html

CHAPTER EIGHT

McKinsey & Company. (2022, October 18). *Women in the workplace 2022.* McKinsey & Company. Retrieved June 1, 2022, from https://

www.mckinsey.com/featured-insights/diversity-and-inclusion/women-in-the-workplace

SHRM. (2022, March 2). *SHRM releases 'women in leadership: Unequal access on the journey to the top'*. SHRM. Retrieved June 1, 2022, from https://www.shrm.org/about-shrm/press-room/press-releases/pages/

Women, leadership, and the priority paradox. IBM. (2019). Retrieved June 19, 2022, from https://www.ibm.com/thought-leadership/institute-business-value/report/womeninleadership

Sponsorship and mentoring: Ask catalyst express. Catalyst. (2022, August 29). Retrieved June 27, 2022, from https://www.catalyst.org/research/sponsorship-and-mentoring-ask-catalyst-express/

Saperstein, S. R. (2022, January 24). *How to find a sponsor to boost your career*. Time.com. Retrieved June 22, 2022, from https://time.com/charter/6130567/sponsor-mentor-career/

Melvin, C., & BlancAccen, J. (2020). *Women sponsorship drives innovation | accenture*. Accenture.com. Retrieved June 18, 2022, from https://www.accenture.com/_acnmedia/PDF-119/Accenture-Sponsorship-Women-Drives-Innovation.pdf

Perez, T. (2019, July 31). *Sponsors: Valuable allies not everyone has*. Payscale. Retrieved June 17, 2022, from https://www.payscale.com/research-and-insights/mentorship-sponsorship-benefits/

The surprising benefits of sponsoring others at work. Harvard Business Review. (2019, July 18). Retrieved June 8, 2022, from https://hbr.org/podcast/2019/06/the-surprising-benefits-of-sponsoring-others-at-work

Anderson, R. H., & Smith, D. G. (2019, August 7). *What men can do to be better mentors and sponsors to women*. Harvard Business Review. Retrieved June 17, 2022, from https://hbr.org/2019/08/what-men-can-do-to-be-better-mentors-and-sponsors-to-women

Hewlett, S. A. (2019, June 17). *Want to be a better manager? get a protégé.* Harvard Business Review. Retrieved June 9, 2022, from https://hbr.org/2019/06/want-to-be-a-better-manager-get-a- protege

Ibarra, H. (2019, August 19). *A lack of sponsorship is keeping women from advancing into leadership.* Harvard Business Review. Retrieved June 26, 2022, from https://hbr.org/2019/08/a-lack-of-sponsorship-is-keeping-women-from-advancing-into-leadership

Sancier-Sultan, S., Sperling-Magro, J., & Garibian, D. (2019, November 29). *Taking the lead for inclusion.* McKinsey & Company. Retrieved June 15, 2022, from https://www.mckinsey.com/featured-insights/gender-equality/taking-the-lead-for-inclusion

Hutson, M. (2018, October 5). *Why are there so few female leaders?* Scientific American. Retrieved June 8, 2022, from https://www.scientificamerican.com/article/why-are-there-so-few-female-leaders/

Women in management (quick take). Catalyst. (2022, March 1). Retrieved June 16, 2022, from https://www.catalyst.org/research/women-in-management/

Why diversity and inclusion matter: Financial performance (appendix). Catalyst. (2020, June 24). Retrieved June 27, 2022, from https://www.catalyst.org/research/why-diversity-and-inclusion-matter-financial-performance/

Werner, L. (2022, February 23). *How to help women overcome burnout at work.* DDI. Retrieved June 21, 2022, from https://www.ddi-world.com/blog/overcome-burnout

Women in the workplace 2022. LeanIn.Org and McKinsey & Company. (2022). Retrieved June 9, 2022, from https://womenintheworkplace.com/

Gallup. (2020). *Perspective on employee burnout: Causes and cures.* Gallup.com. Retrieved June 23, 2022, from https://www.gallup.com/workplace/282659/employee-burnout-perspective-paper.aspx

Wigert, B. (2020, March 13). *Employee burnout: The biggest myth.* Gallup.com. Retrieved June 15, 2022, from https://www.gallup. com/workplace/288539/employee-burnout-biggest-myth.aspx

Sanner, B., & Evans, K. (2021, April 8). *Do the words "Performance review" scare you?* Harvard Business Review. Retrieved June 7, 2022, from https://hbr.org/2021/04/do-the-words-performanc e-review-scare-you

Burns, T., Huang, J., Krivkovich, A., Rambachan, I., Trkulja, T., Yee, L., & Yee, L. (2021, October 22). *Women do more to fight burnout - and it's burning them out.* Harvard Business Review. Retrieved June 13, 2022, from https://hbr.org/2021/10/women-do-more-t o-fight-burnout-and-its-burning-them-out

Van Bommel, T. (2022, November 11). *The power of empathy in times of crisis and beyond (report).* Catalyst. Retrieved June 21, 2022, from https://www.catalyst.org/reports/empathy-work-strategy-crisis/

Twaronite, K. (2019, February 28). *The surprising power of simply asking coworkers how they're doing.* Harvard Business Review. Retrieved June 18, 2022, from https://hbr.org/2019/02/the-surprisin g-power-of-simply-asking-coworkers-how-theyre-doing

Coffman, J., Bax, B., Noether, A., & Blair, B. (2022, March 31). *The fabric of belonging: How to weave an inclusive culture.* Bain. Retrieved June 23, 2022, from https://www.bain.com/insights/the-fabric-o f-belonging-how-to-weave-an-inclusive-culture/

Ellsworth, D., Goldstein, D., & Schaninger, B. (2021, February 16). *Inclusion doesn't happen by accident: Measuring Inclusion in a way that matters.* McKinsey & Company. Retrieved June 27, 2022, from https://www.mckinsey.com/capabili- ties/people-and-organizational-performance/our-insights/ the-organization-blog/inclusion-doesnt-happen-by-accide nt-measuring-inclusion-in-a-way-that-matters

CHAPTER NINE

Sandberg, D. J. (2019, October 16). *When women lead, firms win - spglobal.com*. SPGlobal.com. Retrieved August 3, 2022, from https://www.spglobal.com/_division_assets/images/ special-editorial/iif-2019/whenwomenlead.pdf

Wechsler, P. (2015, March 3). *Women-led companies perform three times better than the S&P 500*. Fortune. Retrieved July 19, 2022, from https://fortune.com/2015/03/03/women-led-companies-perfor m-three-times-better-than-the-sp-500/

Post, C., Lokshin, B., & Boone, C. (2021, April 6). *Research: Adding women to the C-suite changes how companies think*. Harvard Business Review. Retrieved August 14, 2022, from https://hbr. org/2021/04/research-adding-women-to-the-c-suite-change s-how-companies-think

Torry, H. (2022, March 13). *Women embrace flexible working, but economists say it could hinder their careers*. The Wall Street Journal. Retrieved August 16, 2022, from https://www.wsj.com/articles/ women-embrace-flexible-working-but-economists-say-it-could -hinder-their-careers-11647180001?mod=hp_lead_pos7

Key findings from women in the workplace 2021. Lean In. (2021). Retrieved July 28, 2021, from https://leanin.org/ women-in-the-workplace-2021

Gurchiek, K. (2021, March 8). *Flexible work options, career development can keep women in the workforce*. SHRM. Retrieved July 15, 2022, from https://www.shrm.org/resourcesandtools/hr-topics/ behavioral-competencies/global-and-cultural-effectiveness/ pages/flexible-work-options-career-development-can-ke ep-women-in-the-workforce-.aspx

Johnson, W. B., & Smith, D. G. (2021, October 11). *Advancing gender equity as you lead out of the pandemic.* Harvard Business Review. Retrieved August 18, 2022, from https://hbr.org/2021/10/advancing-gender-equity-as-you-lead-out-of-the-pandemic

Make the invisible visible: Catalyst #biascorrect for International Women's day 2021 campaign asks Challenging Questions (media release). Catalyst. (2021, March 3). Retrieved July 11, 2022, from https://www.catalyst.org/media-release/bias-correct-iwd-2021/

Barroso, A., & Brown, A. (2021, May 25). *Gender pay gap in U.S. held steady in 2020.* Pew Research Center. Retrieved August 7, 2022, from https://www.pewresearch.org/fact-tank/2021/05/25/gender-pay-gap-facts/

Bleiweis, R., Frye, J., & Khattar, R. (2021, November 17). *Women of color and the wage gap.* Center for American Progress. Retrieved August 18, from https://www.americanprogress.org/article/women-of-color-and-the-wage-gap/

Hernandez, J. (2022, May 18). *The U.S. Men's and women's soccer teams will be paid equally under a new deal.* NPR. Retrieved August 7, 2022, from https://www.npr.org/2022/05/18/1099697799/us-soccer-equal-pay-agreement-women

U.S. Soccer Federation, women's and men's national team unions agree to historic collective bargaining agreements. US Soccer.com. (2022, May 18). Retrieved August 7, 2022, from https://www.ussoccer.com/stories/2022/05/ussf-womens-and-mens-national-team-unions-agree-to-historic-collective-bargaining-agreements

Women are paid less than men-and the gap is closing too slowly. Lean In. (n.d.). Retrieved August 8, 2022, from https://leanin.org/equal-pay-data-about-the-gender-pay-gap

Frye, J. V. (2021, March 24). *10 essential actions to promote equal pay.* Center for American Progress. Retrieved August 23, 2022, from https://www.americanprogress.org/article/10-essential-actions-promote-equal-pay/

Nagele-Piazza, L. (2020, February 21). *The importance of pay equity.* SHRM. Retrieved August 10, 2022, from https://www.shrm.org/hr-today/news/hr-magazine/spring2020/pages/importance-of-pay-equity.aspx

JUST Capital 23% of the largest U.S. companies analyze their gender pay gaps. JUST Capital. (2022, March 15). Retrieved August 17, 2022, from https://justcapital.com/news/equal-pay-day-2022-companies-analyzing-gender-wage-gaps/

Gender equality in the U.S. - Equileap. (2020). Retrieved July 30, 2022, from https://equileap.com/wp-content/uploads/2020/12/Equileap_US_Report_2020.pdf

Tell the world about WRN. GM Women's Retail Network. (n.d.). Retrieved July 30, 2022, from https://www.gmwomensretailnetwork.com/key-messages/

LaReau, J. L. (2021, March 25). *GM just became only automaker with Board of Directors that's majority women.* Detroit Free Press. Retrieved July 30, 2022, from https://www.freep.com/story/money/cars/general-motors/2021/03/25/gm-board-women-diversity-meg-whitman-mark-tatum/6969922002/

Andrews, J. (2020) *Closing the gap on Gender Equality, G20 Magazine.* Available at: https://digital.thecatcompanyinc.com/g7magazine/france-2019/closing-the-gap-on-gender-equality/ (Accessed: July 21, 2022).

Equileap (2019) *Landing Page Global Report Form.* Available at: https://info.equileap.com/2019genderequalityglobalreportandranking (Accessed: August 11, 2022).

L'Oréal selected as the top gender-balanced company by Equileap. Mirror Review. (2018, October 4). Retrieved August 17, 2022, from https://www.mirrorreview.com/loreal-selected-as-the-top-gender-balanced-company-by-equileap/

At Nielsen, we #choosetochallenge. Nielsen. (2021, March 28). Retrieved August 11, 2022, from https://www.nielsen.com/news-center/2021/at-nielsen-we-choosetochallenge/

Equileap - Official Website. (2022). Retrieved August 10, 2022, from https://equileap.com/wp-content/uploads/2022/03/Equileap_Global_Report_2022.pdf

CHAPTER TEN

Zenger, J., & Folkman, J. (2020, December 30). *Research: Women are better leaders during a crisis.* Harvard Business Review. Retrieved September 29, 2022, from https://hbr.org/2020/12/research-women-are-better-leaders-during-a-crisis

BBC. (2020, April 20). *Coronavirus: How New Zealand relied on science and empathy.* BBC News. Retrieved September 14, 2022, from https://www.bbc.com/news/world-asia-52344299

Harte, C. A., & Vani, S. (2021, July 21). *Jacinda Ardern's rise to power as 'the strong woman'-not the strongman.* Ms. Magazine. Retrieved September 13, from https://msmagazine.com/2021/07/21/jacinda-ardern-women-politics/

Ainge Roy, E. (2020, December 20). *Jacinda Ardern: I try to turn self-doubt into 'something more positive'.* The Guardian. Retrieved September 3, 2022, from https://www.theguardian.com/world/2020/dec/21/jacinda-ardern-i-try-to-turn-self-doubt-into-something-more-positive

BBC. (2020, October 17). *Jacinda Ardern: New Zealand's prime minister.* BBC News. Retrieved September 23, 2022, from https://www.bbc.com/news/world-asia-54565381

Nagesh, A. (2019, March 21). *Jacinda Ardern: 'a leader with love on full display'*. BBC News. Retrieved September 13, 2022, from https://www.bbc.com/news/world-asia-47630129

Underwood, T. (2022, January 19). *The case for a new generation of leaders: Jacinda Ardern*. Harvard Political Review. Retrieved September 13, 2022, from https://harvardpolitics.com/ardern-new-leaders/

Malala's story. Malala Fund. (n.d.). Retrieved September 23, 2022, from https://malala.org/malalas-story

Wikimedia Foundation. (2022, November 19). *Malala Yousafzai*. Wikipedia. Retrieved September 13, 2022, from https://en.wikipedia.org/wiki/Malala_Yousafzai

Nichols, M. (2013, July 12). *Pakistan's Malala, shot by Taliban, takes education plea to U.N.* Reuters. Retrieved September 23, 2022, from https://www.reuters.com/article/us-malala-un-idUSBRE96B0IC20130712

Tapper, A. P. (2017, October 31). *I'm 10. and I want girls to raise their hands*. The New York Times. Retrieved September 9, 2022, from https://www.nytimes.com/2017/10/31/opinion/im-10-and-i-want-girls-to-raise-their-hands.html

GSCNC. (2019, March 11). *Raise your hand | GSCNC*. YouTube. Retrieved September 21, 2022, from https://www.youtube.com/watch?v=2_55o-V8-b0

11-year-old encourages girls to "raise your hand!" with new girl scouts patch and picture book. kwww.amightygirl.com. (2019, March 21). Retrieved September 18, 2022, from https://www.amightygirl.com/blog?p=23696

RESOURCES

Magazine, I. (2019, September 25). *Inc.. founders project with alexa von tobel: How to create change, with Carolyn Childers and Lindsay Kaplan of chief on Apple Podcasts.* Apple Podcasts. Retrieved October 1, 2022, from https://podcasts.apple.com/us/podcast/how-to-create-change-with-carolyn-childers

Deutch, G. (2021, June 2). *The company bringing together female chief executives.* Jewish Insider. Retrieved September 30, 2022, from https://jewishinsider.com/2021/06/chief-company-lindsay-kaplan/

Women have always been powerful. Chief. (n.d.). Retrieved September 15, 2022, from https://chief.com/

Fostering Women's Leadership & Workplace Inclusion. Lean In. (n.d.). Retrieved October 1, 2022, from https://leanin.org/

Behind every woman is a circle of women. make it official. Lean In. (n.d.). Retrieved September 23, 2022, from https://leanin.org/circles

Newman, J. (2018, March 16). *'Lean in': Five years later.* The New York Times. Retrieved September 23, 2022, from https://www.nytimes.com/2018/03/16/business/lean-in-five-years-later.html

About. Lean In. (n.d.). Retrieved September 15, 2022, from https://leanin.org/about

Alliance, T. W. I. (n.d.). *About Us.* The Women's Impact Alliance (WIA). Retrieved October 2, 2022, from https://thewia.org/about/

Alliance, T. W. I. (n.d.). *Unlocked – The book.* The Women's Impact Alliance (WIA). Retrieved October 2, 2022, from https://thewia.org/book/

About women together. Women Together. (n.d.). Retrieved September 30, 2022, from https://womentogether.com/about-women-together/

Home. Women Together. (n.d.). Retrieved September 30, 2022, from https://womentogether.com/

Home. Girls Who Code. (n.d.). Retrieved September 26, 2022, from https://girlswhocode.com/

Public policy. Girls Who Code. (n.d.). Retrieved September 26, 2022, from https://girlswhocode.com/about-us/public-policy

Girls who code. (2019). Retrieved October 3, 2022, from https://girlswhocode.com/wp-content/uploads/2019/06/GWC_Advocacy_2019K12Report_PDF-min-1.pdf

Saujani, R. (2016). *Teach girls bravery, not perfection.* Reshma Saujani: Teach girls bravery, not perfection | TED Talk. Retrieved September 27, 2022, from https://www.ted.com/talks/reshma_saujani_teach_girls_bravery_not_perfection

Biography

Heather Backstrom is an accomplished coach, facilitator, and speaker. Her professional experiences span organizations in the for profit, not for profit and public sector arenas. She coaches leaders at all levels including C-suite, vice president, director, and manager. With a passion for learning she is also an adjunct professor at the University of Redlands.

She is passionate about cultivating empowered women leaders, and that is the inspiration behind *Collaborative Confidence*. She wants all women to confidently use their voice and project their influence, while doing the same for other women.

She loves to learn and have fun at the same time and incorporates proven principles from improv into her work. As a student of improv, she has trained at the Second City, iO West, Upright Citizens Brigade, Bay Area Theater Sports, and Improv LA.

She enjoys traveling and has had the great fortune to float on the Dead Sea, walk on the Great Wall of China, and ride in a hot air balloon over Stockholm, Sweden.

Heather has a M.S. in human resources from Chapman University and a doctorate in organizational leadership from Pepperdine University.

www.heatherbackstrom.com